Your
Horoscope
2020

. . . .

Leo

Your Horoscope 2020

Leo

23rd July - 23rd August

igloobooks

igloobooks

Published in 2019
by Igloo Books Ltd
Cottage Farm
Sywell
NN6 0BJ
www.igloobooks.com

0819 001.01
2 4 6 8 10 9 7 5 3 1
ISBN 978-1-78905-714-0

Written by Belinda Campbell and Denise Evans

Cover design by Dave Chapman
Edited by Bobby Newlyn-Jones

Printed and manufactured in China

CONTENTS
· · · · · · · · · · · · · · · · · ·

INTRODUCTION
··················

This horoscope has been specifically created to allow
you to get the most from astrological patterns and
the way they have a bearing on not only your zodiac
sign, but nuances within it. Using the diary section
of the book you can read about the influences and
possibilities of each and every day of the year. It will
be possible for you to see when you are likely to be
cheerful and happy or those times when your nature
is in retreat and you will be more circumspect. The
diary will help to give you a feel for the specific
'cycles' of astrology and the way they can subtly
change your day-to-day life.

THE CHARACTER OF THE LION

A Fire sign ruled by the Sun was surely destined to always burn the brightest. Like a moth to a flame, people are naturally drawn to Leonians. Whether singing on a stage, dancing in a club or playing football in the park, they dominate every situation by demanding attention and adoration. Born in the fifth house in the zodiac calendar that represents pleasure and creativity, Leonians often derive immense satisfaction and a sense of purpose from making others happy. These fiery lions can be brimming with confidence or struggle with a lack thereof, and need to be validated with constant praise. The laughter of others is like music to their ears and a career in comedy, like fellow Leonians David Walliams and Jo Brand, could be their calling.

Born in the middle of summer, Leo is a fixed sign that works hard at making dreams become a reality. Daring Leonians Amelia Earhart, Neil Armstrong and Barack Obama achieved historical firsts when realising their dreams. Courageous and not averse to taking risks, fortune definitely favours brave Lions. Second place was not invented for these gold-medal fans. Leonians can be competitive to a fault and should remember that there is more to life than winning. At times, they are exhausting to behold, but fortunately there is plenty to love. What they lack in modesty, Leonians make up for in loyalty and are known for being fiercely committed to loved ones and personal goals. At their best, these charismatic leaders rule with a generous heart and visionary mind.

THE LION

It's hard to miss Leonians when they proudly stride into a room. These beings are the kings and queens of their jungle and expect to be treated as such. Give Leonians the royal treatment and they'll be purring sweetly. However, contradict or disrespect them, and get ready to hear their roar. This sign is fierce but loyal. As true leaders of their pack, Leonians can readily be relied on by their loved ones for giving guidance or doing a favour. Strength and courage are usually the Leonian approach, but they also have a side as soft and beautiful as a Lion's mane. The body part associated with Leo is the heart, and these Lions have big ones. Romance from Leonians will be dramatic and bold. Their lovers should expect to be serenaded in the street or proposed to via a message written in the sky. Go big or go home could be the Leonian mantra, because they were not born to blend into the masses.

THE SUN

The Sun sits at the centre of the universe, and those born under the sign of Leo naturally assume the same position. This makes them charismatic and popular, and, just like the Sun, their absence is felt on days when they are not around. Conversely, there are times when Leonians blaze too forcefully, and those around them must seek shade! However, Leonians can heal just as they can hurt. Apollo is known as one of the Greek gods of the Sun, recognised in part for his ability to heal and protect. Apollo was also associated with music and the arts, a contributing factor perhaps to why this Sun-led sign is drawn to taking centre stage. Whether it's pursuing a creative career in the arts or not, the Sun's influence means Leonians usually have a strong sense of who they are and where they are going in life.

ELEMENTS, MODES AND POLARITIES

Each sign is made up of a unique combination of three defining groups: elements, modes and polarities. Each of these defining parts can manifest in good and bad ways, and none should be seen to be a positive or a negative – including the polarities! Just like a jigsaw puzzle, piecing these groups together can help illuminate why each sign has certain characteristics and help us find a balance.

ELEMENTS

Fire: Dynamic and adventurous, signs with Fire in them can be extrovert characters that others are naturally drawn to because of the positive light they give off and their high levels of energy and confidence.

Earth: Signs with the Earth element are steady and driven with their ambitions and make for a solid friend, parent or partner due to their grounded influence and nurturing nature.

Air: The invisible element that influences each of the other elements significantly, Air signs will provide much needed perspective to others with their fair thinking, verbal skills and key ideas.

Water: Warm in the shallows and freezing as ice. This mysterious element is essential to the growth of everything around it, through its emotional depth and empathy.

MODES

Cardinal: Pioneers of the calendar, cardinal signs jump-start each season and are the energetic go-getters.

Fixed: Marking the middle of the calendar, fixed signs firmly denote and value steadiness and reliability.

Mutable: As the seasons end, the mutable signs adapt and give themselves over gladly to the promise of change.

POLARITIES

Positive: Typically extroverted, positive signs take physical action and embrace outside stimulus in their life.

Negative: Usually introverted, negative signs value emotional development and experiencing life from the inside out.

LEONIANS IN BRIEF

The table below shows the key attributes of Leonians. Use it for quick reference and to understand more about this fascinating sign.

SYMBOL	RULING PLANET	MODE	ELEMENT	HOUSE
The Lion	The Sun	Fixed	Fire	Fifth

COLOUR	BODY PART	POLARITY	GENDER	POLAR SIGN
Purple, Gold	Heart and Spine	Positive	Masculine	Aquarius

LOVE

....

Leonians are associated with the heart, which is perhaps why they appear to love being in love. They take great pleasure in moving heaven and Earth to romance the socks off their love interests. A Bridget Jones-style kiss in the snow or even standing at the front of a ship like Jack and Rose, these brave Lions will romance their partners as good as any romcom movie character. Whether such bold statements of love appeal is a question of personal taste, yet it's difficult not to fall head over heels for these charismatic charmers.

Leonians are the performers of the calendar and have no problem having all admiring eyes on them. Throw roses at their feet and they will likely provide an encore. Clap too enthusiastically, however, and the Leonian ego may take over. They appreciate partners that shower them with praise, but they should try not to demand it. Practising modesty and channelling a quieter confidence can make Leonians even more charming.

Although the demands of Leonians in love can be great, they will give themselves wholeheartedly to their partners. No expense will be spared in their generous gestures of romance, but it will be their staggering displays of loyalty that will probably be appreciated the most. Once they have set their sights on someone, they will be honest and faithful until the end. Leonians have a fearless approach to love, which can mean that they open themselves up to plenty of heartbreak. Yet their courage is contagious, and their willingness to take risks can lead to the biggest rewards in love.

ARIES: COMPATIBILITY 2/5

Arians are used to being first, but they'll have to learn to
share the spotlight and decision-making if they fall for
a leader of the jungle. These two signs should recognise
clearly their similarities, and therefore know just how to
advise and support one another in reaching their goals.
With the Leonian led by the heart and the Arian by the
head, arguments can be a roaring battlefield when these
two don't see eye to eye. Ego and pride will need to be
kept in check on both sides if this relationship is to go
the distance.

TAURUS: COMPATIBILITY 3/5

Leo is ruled by the Sun and Taurus by Venus; this star
and planet are never further away than 48 degrees from
each other. The love that these two share is solidified in
their sometimes-stubborn commitment to one another.
The Lion and Bull are both fixed signs, and this can be
their undoing in a long-term relationship when neither
one is willing to compromise. Both the Lion and Bull
will shower each other with affection and admiration,
and will boost each other's self-esteem and be a positive
influence in their careers. This couple should just be
careful to not let their egos get in the way.

GEMINI: COMPATIBILITY 4/5

The inner Leonian child can be just what the youthful
sign of Gemini asked for. This love can be like a
children's story full of love and adventure, think Peter
Pan and Wendy. The high-energy Leonian was born

to lead, whilst the mutable Geminian is happy to take this Lion's hand and fly speedily off to Neverland! The Leonian will encourage the Geminian to take an active part in the important choices in their lives. Both positive signs, their extrovert energies and curious natures will see this Air and Fire match embarking on endless adventures.

CANCER: COMPATIBILITY 1/5

Leo is ruled by the Sun and Cancer by the Moon, so this pairing can feel as different as night and day. However, the Lion and the Crab can also find that they have plenty in common to form a lasting love. Born in the fourth and fifth houses that partly signify family and children, the Leonian and Cancerian share a fundamental desire to find that long-term partner to settle down with. Security is essential for the Cancerian and the fixed side of the steadfast Leonian can provide just that. This power couple could go the distance if their differences are embraced.

LEO: COMPATIBILITY 3/5

When a Leonian loves a Leonian, it's like stars colliding and causing a supernova explosion. Beautiful and dramatic, these two creatives are naturally pulled together. With so many Leonians using their talents for the dramatics in the arts, this fiery partnership could readily spark on the set of a movie or from working together in some other creative industry. Actors Ben Affleck and Jennifer Lopez are a prime example. However, like with Affleck and Lopez, a long future together is not always guaranteed. Whilst the fun and romance will be plenty, these two fixed signs may struggle to cooperate.

VIRGO: COMPATIBILITY 2/5

The love of a Leonian can take a Virgoan by surprise; which isn't something the introverted Virgoan is always keen on. The clear differences between the studious Virgoan and show-stopping Leonian can mean that these two might be quick to write each other off as potential partners at first glance. The relationship between this Fire and Earth couple can be a slow burner, but their slow and steady approach could well end up with these two winning the race hand in hand. This couple's strengths are their differences, and these two hard workers can make for a solid and complementary couple.

LIBRA: COMPATIBILITY 4/5

Sitting two places apart on the calendar, a Libran and Leonian can share a compatible partnership. The Libran is an expert in diplomacy, so will likely be able to handle the more dramatic moments in this love affair without bruising the Leonian's ego. Love with the Leonian can be a roller coaster, fun but also consisting of ups and downs. The Libran, symbolised by scales, will hopefully bring a balance to the relationship that the reliable Leonian will appreciate. Ruled by the Sun and Venus, the Leonian and Libran are capable of forming a relationship that is filled with warmth and love.

SCORPIO: COMPATIBILITY 1/5

The love between a watery Scorpian and fiery Leonian can be one of deep intimacy or dampened spirits. Here are two fixed signs that could clash in their different approaches, as they refuse to yield to each other's strong personalities. Shared assets, particularly money, could prove difficult for them. The Scorpian is born in the eighth house where shared possessions are important, and the Leonian belongs in the fourth house where a love of gambling resides. This could result in serious conflict for the couple. If respect is exercised regularly between these two lovers, theirs is a closeness well worth protecting.

SAGITTARIUS: COMPATIBILITY 4/5

This Fire sign match will surely spark with excitement.
Here is a couple in which both partners are likely to
plan a surprise romantic getaway for the other with little
or no notice. Both spontaneous and adventurous, the
Leonian and Sagittarian match each other with their
positive energies. They are probably the dynamic couple
that is at the top of every party invite list. It's not all
glittering events, though. The philosophical Sagittarian
and purpose-led Leonian can share a powerful bond,
with an influence that is felt beyond just them.

CAPRICORN: COMPATIBILITY 4/5

A Leonian and Capricornian are the success love story
of when opposites attract. Both tend to have a clear
sense of purpose. For the Leonian, it is in their personal
life, and for the Capricornian it is in their career.
Leonian Barack Obama and Capricornian Michelle
Obama are an ideal example of how well these two
can work towards achieving their dreams together. The
Capricornian can show the Leonian what hard work
can accomplish, and the Leonian can bring the fun that
sometimes the cool and dignified Capricornian can be
lacking. These are two very strong characters that can be
even stronger together.

AQUARIUS: COMPATIBILITY 5/5

Aquarius is the Air sign that sparks the embers of Leo's Fire element into full blaze. Opposites on the calendar, this combination of shared positive energy, fixed attitudes and complimentary elements makes for two individuals that were astrologically meant to be. These unique characters can be guilty of feeling superior to others, so may need to remind themselves to treat each other as their rightful equals. Foremost, this is a friendship sprung from fun and crafted by a shared creativity. The visionary mind of the Leonian combined with the Aquarian's ideals could have these two creating a utopic life together.

PISCES: COMPATIBILITY 2/5

When a Leonian meets a Piscean, they can bring out the best and worst in each other. The Piscean can be a source of emotional encouragement for the Leonian, whilst the Leonian could help the dreamy Piscean take more action in their life to fully realise dreams. Born in the twelfth house representing sacrifice, the Piscean can be selfless. The Sun-ruled Leonian can be the opposite. When these two sacrificing and self-serving characteristics are felt at their extremes, the relationship can turn toxic. However, the mutable Piscean and fixed Leonian can live in harmony if they both value each other's best qualities.

FAMILY AND FRIENDS

All great leaders have a loyal following of subjects, and intrepid Leonians are no exception. Like the Sun, they have the power to draw their friends and families outside so that they can spend time in their warm embrace. Being around heartfelt Lions can lift people's spirits and bring huge amounts of fun and joy. Their outgoing and extroverted energy can be contagious, but it can also be tiring. Fellow positive signs could make for great high-energy friends that can easily keep up with these social butterflies. More introverted negative signs can also play an important role. A friend or family member that Leonians do not constantly have to perform for offer an important change of pace, and an opportunity to recharge.

For all the love and support that Leonians receive from their family and friends, they will give back threefold. They are most known for their unparalleled generosity. Leonians love luxury, so their gifts can be extravagant, whether they have the cash to spoil their loved ones or not. If their bank accounts aren't quite big enough to indulge friends, Leonians can be creative even on the most frugal of budgets. Leonians will share money if they have it but, more importantly, they will always give their valued time and energy to relationships.

Belonging to the fifth house in the calendar that is closely associated with children, the protective and high-spirited Leonian can make a wonderful, and empathetic, parent. In some ways, Leonians never grow up so can remember the frustrations of being young. Their inner children will bring the fun and energy required into raising offspring, or they will be the fun aunt or uncle that their nieces and nephews always want to play with. If Leonians do not have children of their own, other people's will no doubt still gravitate towards them. This makes Leonians the go-to babysitter or first choice of godparent.

Whilst sunny Leonians can have a warm and healing quality, their stage-hogging presence can be overpowering and destructive to their relationships. Their presence and roar is as loud as a Lion's, and it risks drowning out everyone else. It may not be the intention of Leonians to overshadow their friends and family, but the self-led influence from their guiding Sun can turn this confident ruler into a bossy dictator. Their fixed attitudes can make them resistant to the different opinions of others, but Leonians should be careful of surrounding themselves with only yes-men. A diverse social network where everyone has a voice is the only kingdom worthy of Leonian leadership.

MONEY AND CAREERS

· · · · · · · · · · · · · · · · · ·

Being a particular star sign will not dictate that you follow a certain type of career, but it can help you to identify potential areas for thriving in. Conversely, to succeed in the workplace, it is just as important to understand strengths and weaknesses to achieve career and financial goals.

A love for luxury and aristocratic tendencies creates a risk for Leonians to become too focused on the material things in life. It can be good to enjoy a little luxury in life, as long as they don't let it dominate everything they do. However, if they can channel their love for grand things creatively, they could follow in the footsteps of notable Leonian fashion designers such as Yves Saint-Laurent, Coco Chanel and Michael Kors. Rather than wearing the designer names of others, Leonians possess a passion for luxury and leadership that could help them become the next big name that everyone is coveting.

Whilst Leonians enjoy the best in life, they will generally be sensible with their finances and not spend beyond their means. A trip to Vegas might be tempting, but they aren't usually the type to go for broke and risk losing it all. The fixed part of Leonians will keep their spending steady, unwilling to risk losing their financial security. They may be driven to earn lots of money so that they can buy all the luxuries they desire, but they will probably earn their fortune through organised efforts and a steadfast approach rather than at the slot machines.

Whether Leonians go for the leading roles in a film or strive after leading a country, they will be comfortable in the spotlight of their choice. Leonians' natural self-assurance makes them authoritative and confident figures, and others will respect that, if given the opportunity. So whether it's the moves of Leonian Mick Jagger or the skills of David Beckham, all eyes will be firmly on them.

If fame doesn't appeal, managerial roles could be a natural domain in many industries, be it on a football field or in an office. Occupations in the world of luxury are also appealing, given Leonians' appreciation of the finer things in life. But no matter the field, being boss is often the primary goal, although a bossy attitude should to be avoided wherever possible to keep others happy.

As with family, colleagues cannot be chosen. Therefore, it can be advantageous to use star signs to learn about their key characteristics and discover the best ways of working together. Part of the attraction for becoming a leader for Leonians is the competition. The king or queen of the jungle loves to demonstrate their prowess and rise above any competitors. However, Leonians can be dominating and may need to remind themselves that there is no 'I' in 'team', especially if they are working with other 'me first' characters, such as Arians. Taureans might share the same ambitious dreams as Leonians, but any colleague that is also fixed will need to work harder at compromise.

HEALTH AND WELLBEING

These bold Lions can also be highly sensitive souls. Like anyone, they have their ups and downs, so friends and family can be essential supporters that straighten the crown on their ruler's head. The critical words of Virgoans might be felt too harshly by sensitive Leonians, and knock their confidence further if they are already feeling low. Pisceans or Cancerians could tread more carefully, and be the emotionally encouraging friends that help Leonians stride forwards again. A need for constant reassurance can stem from a crisis in confidence, so Leonians should work on building up their own self-esteem from within so that they do not have to always rely on others to lift them out of their low moods. Owning their mistakes and recognising where they can improve are just a couple of ways that Leonians can grow to become happier and humble.

Winning can feel wonderful, but when Leonians reach their desired peak, they may find themselves at a loss. Once Leonians rise to the top of their profession, they may need to take up another hobby or avenue of interest to satisfy their urge to win. Throwing themselves into a competitive sport that takes them outside will appease their ambitious side, youthful energy and love of the Sun. Whilst protection from harmful UV rays is important, spending time in the Sun sensibly can be just as vital for keeping healthy. Apart from receiving essential Vitamin D, sunshine's healing properties also extend to lowering cholesterol and reducing high blood pressure – wonderful news for heart-associated Leonians. Learning lines for their latest play in the sunshine, or swimming in a lido rather than an indoor swimming pool, could also help improve physical and mental health.

Guided by the Sun, representing the self and life purpose, Leonians seem to know who they are and where they are going. At least that's what it can look like from the standpoint of admiring onlookers. If Leonians lack direction in life, it can be a major source of upset for them. They may feel they are not living up to their own expectations or the expectations of others. Leonians should try to take the pressure off themselves, and understand that learning who they truly are and where they wish to get to in life are two big questions that plague everyone. They would do well to cut themselves some slack, and not get bogged down by their reputation of always being the best. The high status of the charismatic, larger than life Lion can be a burden to Leonians that feel they don't fit the bill. They are essentially best at being themselves, whatever form that may take, so should not attempt to cage themselves within the confines of expectation.

Leo

· · · · · · · · · · · · · · · ·

2020
DIARY PAGES

JANUARY

. . . .

Wednesday 1st
Happy New Year! 2020 begins with the Moon in your
sex, death, rebirth and power struggles sector. You
are thinking about endings and beginnings, which is
completely natural for the start of a new year. However,
yours are deep and secretive.

Thursday 2nd
Talkative Mercury is using his enquiring mind in your
health and mundane duties sector to ask Jupiter how
to expand on these issues. You will want to add things
to your daily routines, and may start researching better
health habits or activities where you can help people.

Friday 3rd
Your mood today has a thrilling edge to it. You have
a renewed thirst for adventure and seem to have
researched what is needed to enrich your life. You are
feeling the pull towards distant lands far from home.

Saturday 4th

Your drive this weekend is to have fun and express yourself in ways not previously tried, or tried once but since forgotten. Artistic pursuits appeal now, and your soul is bursting to create something new. You are seeking a meaningful purpose to life.

Sunday 5th

Career and what you may leave behind are on your mind. You're keen to accumulate riches and have some security to fall back on. On the other hand, investing in your future features now. Take a look at career advancement.

Monday 6th

Your mood is moving towards change today. Check out all available resources and how far you can go with transforming something into a more valuable prospect. Consider any limitations carefully, but do not be held back by them.

Tuesday 7th

Change and boundaries will be the theme for this week. Ponder the tasks you do for others and how they impact on your health. Do you give too much of yourself and, if so, is it draining you? How can this be done in a different way?

Wednesday 8th

There is a direct connection between the boundaries you have been thinking about recently and a special person in your life. Venus, the goddess of love, is asking you to consider this person and factor them into your plans too. Making a change together looks promising.

Thursday 9th

The Moon moves into your social sector and you could be gathering information from friends or groups. Research carried out in these areas will be beneficial and provide lots of options for you to choose from. The Moon and Venus are also making a nice connection today for love and romance.

Friday 10th

The Full Moon and lunar eclipse in your dream sector show the multitude of possibilities on offer. You feel nurtured, so safely drift off into your own little world imagining scenarios that nourish and sustain. Spiritual retreats and personal quests attract you now. Family and home also feature today.

Saturday 11th

Your mood continues to be somewhat surreal and you'll prefer to be alone for some of this time. You wonder about how to fit the resulting dreams into your daily life. The idea of doing something courageous appeals to you now.

Sunday 12th

As the Moon drifts into your sign, your mood and outward expression are in sync. Wear your heart on your sleeve and you will attract people who simply enjoy being in your company. You are everybody's number one today, so enjoy it.

Monday 13th

Turn your attention towards your lover or another important person who needs you. Is there something special you could do together? The Sun is sitting with Saturn and Pluto in your health and routine sector, which may shed light about an important change.

Tuesday 14th

Venus moves into your sector of sex, death and rebirth. Here she is the Dark Goddess or the Priestess and can entice you into forbidden or taboo areas. As the Priestess, she is asking you what needs to end before something new can begin.

Wednesday 15th

The Moon is in your area of money and possessions and you could be quite broody about financial security. You will need to look at how everyday activities support or put strain on your resources. Do you spend too much on trips to the supermarket, for example? Could you cut back somewhere?

Thursday 16th

You are now being asked to find harmony in your communications sector, bringing an urgent need to do more research into something connected to your daily routine. Are these one and the same thing? Your love life could bring welcome surprises too. Keep an open mind today.

Friday 17th

There is going to be a lot of listening and talking with your significant other or, indeed, some other important people in your life now. Mercury has moved into this area and he will want to shake things up a bit and maybe start a revolution. Take care to consider needs other than your own.

Saturday 18th

As the Moon moves into your family sector, you
will be engrossed in deep thoughts about ancestry
and your background. Maybe keep those thoughts to
yourself, however, as Mercury is clashing with Uranus
who likes to shock. Lineage and legacy are on your
mind right now.

Sunday 19th

Continuing with yesterday's searching thoughts
about family, you will be contemplating how you may
previously have been restricted or made to play by the
rules, perhaps by a family member. You'll feel the urge to
break free of the norm and rebel.

Monday 20th

The Sun has moved into your opposite sign of Aquarius,
so you should be turning your attention to others
around now. This is usually about a lover or a
significant person in your life, but on this occasion,
for you it is about larger groups. Who is more radical,
you or them?

Tuesday 21st

The Sun is shining its light on you, but it is revealing your shadow. These are the traits you would prefer to be kept hidden or that you dislike about others, which actually exist in you. Now is the time to do some work on this.

Wednesday 22nd

Head versus heart battles surface today. There are things you would like to do for yourself, but other duties just seem to be getting in the way. How can you resolve these issues and maintain some balance in life? The solution isn't always obvious, but it's worth trying to find.

Thursday 23rd

You might be rather irritable now. Your mood and emotions are making issues seem larger than they actually are. Be careful not to react or respond in ways that may cause problems at work. Lie low and this will soon pass.

Friday 24th

A New Moon in your relationship sector may see you making a late new year's resolution. However, it won't be easy to articulate your intentions clearly, as a clash between Venus and Mars is also playing out in your sign. Confusion or conflict could be the result.

Saturday 25th

You have a chance to smooth over any upset from yesterday as Mars connects with Mercury, making straightforward self-expression possible. There will be no beating around the bush as you say exactly what you mean, leaving no room for misunderstandings. It's time to patch things up.

Sunday 26th

Sticking with the recent theme of discussing things nicely, why don't you put your heart into what you are saying? Today is favourable for doing just this and letting people know exactly how you feel, as well as what you think. You will be received well if you do this.

Monday 27th

This is a wonderful day for dreaming or diving as deeply as you can go. As the Moon drifts into your sex, death and rebirth sector, Venus will also get close with Neptune. Dive for pearls and look for the treasure that hides in the deepest part of you or your loved one.

Tuesday 28th

The Moon joins Venus near Neptune, possibly uncovering some of your innermost fears. Pay attention to dreams and symbols at this time, as they are messages for you to listen to and grow from. Deep psychological work can be done now.

Wednesday 29th

After wallowing around in deep waters, you surface
with a fire in your belly and a need for action. You feel a
growing sense of purpose and have great ideas that you
are keen to implement. A courageous you rises now, and
wants to blaze a trail.

Thursday 30th

Before you take any action or make an important
decision, check in with your emotions and look at past
lessons that may help you move forward into your
exciting future. This may feel somewhat restricting or
uncomfortable, but stick with it.

Friday 31st

You may feel despondent and wonder why you ever
had such fantastic ideas that will probably not come to
anything. Feeling down in the dumps will not get things
done. This mood will soon pass, so stay in the planning
stages and be satisfied with that.

FEBRUARY

....

Saturday 1st

The Moon passes into your career sector and you
will need to knuckle back down into what brings you
security. Ask yourself: am I rowing this boat alone? You
may be prone to a tantrum, but trust that your hard
work and dedication will pay off.

Sunday 2nd

Issues of power and control come up today as Venus,
the Goddess of Love, talks to Pluto, the Dark Lord.
All is ultimately well, however, as their meeting brings
an easy conversation in your sector of sex, death and
rebirth. Money talk and shared resources could also be
discussed now.

Monday 3rd

Your social life and friendship groups, whether online
or in person, are in focus now and brainstorming ideas
could bring new perspectives for you. You tend to be
radical and will accept innovative ways of doing things
that at one time you would have ignored.

Tuesday 4th

Let's talk about sex. Mercury has moved into this sector, and is focused on communication, thinking and learning. As he is allowed to enter the Underworld at will, you may shock yourself at how easily you can discuss taboo or risqué subjects. Secrets can be shared now.

Wednesday 5th

You could be quite fearful today. Your recent discussions may now make you feel uncomfortable, and you would rather forget what you have learnt. Fear not. Keep the secrets that have been shared and all will be well. Be discreet.

Thursday 6th

Your urge to retreat is strong. The recent past has gone too quickly and you need to catch your breath, but you will have to do so under the waters of a Cancer Moon. Stay home with comfort foods and familiarity to avoid trouble.

Friday 7th

Venus is at a critical point in your sex sector. Before she moves on, she wants to make sure you fully understand everything that has transpired in the last few weeks she has been there. Let your lover know that you are both on the same page.

Saturday 8th

The Moon enters your sign and you will feel self-conscious, as if everyone is looking at you. This is usually not a problem, but this is coming from your own emotions and has no basis in reality. Turn this around and show yourself the truth.

Sunday 9th

The unease you felt yesterday is because you now have a Full Moon in your sign. It is asking you to step forward as your brave, courageous, heart-centred self. If you lean towards the negative or become narcissistic it will not do you any favours.

Monday 10th

Today is a day where you will need to check in with your finances and look at how money is coming in, as well as how it is going out. You may even think about contributing to the community or volunteering in some way. Donating to charity can make you feel good.

Tuesday 11th

Doing something for someone else without expecting a reward is the brave and selfless thing you can do now. You should also be thinking about your health, while looking at which new fitness programmes would suit you. An upbeat mood fits the day.

Wednesday 12th

Today your leadership qualities are called upon to balance and settle an argument. This could be with other people or within yourself. Short trips and siblings are also a feature, so you may have to be judge and jury but hopefully not the executioner. People are looking up to you.

Thursday 13th

Are you feeling the push and pull of your daily duties? This is simply the Moon causing tension with planets in your routine sector. This will pass, so try not to make any changes on impulse. Consider all the available options and you may not even need to make a choice.

Friday 14th

A Scorpio Moon in your family and home sector means that a Valentine's Night spent under the duvet with your significant other, some nice food and comforts will be all that is required. Staying home is the new sexy. Enjoy it.

Saturday 15th

Today brings a warning about Mercury retrograde, which will begin on the 17th of this month. For you, it means a need to revise and review things that have recently happened in your sex, death and rebirth sector. Also, backup any devices and double-check travel plans.

Sunday 16th

Stealthy Mars moves into your health and duty sector. Any plans you may have had for change here can receive a boost of energy and forward motion. Mars likes exercise, so this would be an ideal time to start a new fitness regime.

Monday 17th

Mercury retrograde begins. Be very careful with anything concerning secrets now because Mercury may want to reveal all, which could prove detrimental. Try not to make any commitments, as they are unlikely to materialise at this time.

Tuesday 18th

Dreams are getting bigger, but so are illusions. Today you may want to drift off into a fantasy land but be warned, all that glitters is not gold. Be careful not to self-medicate with unhealthy foods or alcohol, and instead be sensible about how you look after yourself. Switch off in safe-mode.

Wednesday 19th

The Sun now enters the sector of your life that has been highlighted strongly this year – sex, death and rebirth. You may see issues with greater clarity or want to indulge more in life's pleasures. It is up to you, but remember that problematic Mercury retrograde resides in the same area.

Thursday 20th

Your emotions are mixed. You may want to expand on some areas in your duties and health sector, or you may also want to cut back and take on less. You are the one in control here, and it is your health that matters. Overdo things and you will pay for it.

Friday 21st

Volatile Mars is working up a sweat in your health house, but his connection with Uranus means he should burn out and fade away. This will allow you to go beyond your personal borders and surprise yourself. Take it easy and be careful.

Saturday 22nd

The Moon moves into your relationship sector, so you could be moody and emotional. This can bring out a narcissistic streak, and you'll want to be the centre of attention. Now is not your time. Focus on your relationships and all will be well.

Sunday 23rd

A New Moon occurs today in your sex, death and rebirth sector. You not only get a chance to make mini-resolutions, but you'll also be able to look at the resources you share with someone. What needs to end and what needs to begin?

Monday 24th

Venus and Jupiter, the two nicer planets, are not at ease with each other today. Venus, as the Warrior Goddess in your travel sector, is blocked, and cannot move ahead without the watchful eye of Jupiter. Who is preventing you from moving on with your plans?

Tuesday 25th

You are reviewing your health and any new fitness programmes you have started. Are they working? Do you feel any better for them? Have a look at what may have worked in the past and what skills you have brought with you.

Wednesday 26th

Mercury is not only retrograde but has absolutely nothing to say. Communications around sex could be blocked or dismissed. You may also find that people do not want to listen to what you have to say on the subject. It is best to be like Mercury and stay quiet today.

Thursday 27th

What you desire and what you feel is needed come into question. You will be making a review of your health and duty and asking if your current activities are nourishing or draining you. Do you love what you do or are you doing it because it is expected?

Friday 28th

You will be moody about your career status today. You plod on and commit to your task list, but is it really getting you anywhere? You are reliable and dependable at work, but is this really what you want?

Saturday 29th

You are continuing to think about your career. You may have a problem with those in charge and speak your mind. You want better from your job and are asking for it, but it is not forthcoming. What can be done about this?

MARCH

....

Sunday 1st

Today is an easy day and you will be quietly contemplating issues surrounding health and duties. For now, you are satisfied with plodding on but know there is something more out there. Just keep your nose to the grind, your head down and focus.

Monday 2nd

The Moon, now in your social sector, means that you feel the need to be with friends and like-minded folk. This could also be online in social media groups where you feel happy expressing views that in some circles could be seen as antagonistic. Say what you like today.

Tuesday 3rd

Views expressed yesterday are making you feel good today. You will feel valued as part of a team or group, knowing that your input is appreciated. You will also feel less lonely and have an established sense of tribe around you.

Wednesday 4th

Mercury moves back into your sector concerning relationships and significant others. Be careful not to upset anyone with unchecked words. Remember to ask yourself if it is true, kind and necessary. Meanwhile, the Moon allows you to dream a little.

Thursday 5th

You would like to just float away and be left in peace. This is what your mind wants, but your body needs to get moving and do some physical exercise. You are not in sync with yourself today. Venus now enters your career house and may bring some harmony in that area for you.

Friday 6th

The need for structure and change in your daily routine is on your mind. You want to shake it all up but cannot see how to do so. You encounter many rules and restrictions that you must abide by, leaving you feeling resentful.

Saturday 7th

Your emotional needs turn towards yourself. As you know, this can mean your ego will get bigger and you'll want to be the star of the show. It would instead be better to demonstrate excellent leadership qualities to those around you.

Sunday 8th

Venus in your career sector bumps into Uranus, who likes surprises. Normally they would not be pleasant ones, but Venus' influence may bring you something sweet and unexpected today. Fantasies and sexual issues may be exposed and could fall apart in front of your eyes. They could also be acted upon.

Monday 9th

Today you have a Full Moon in your money sector. You can now take a good look at what has come to you regarding money and possessions, and what now needs to go. Balancing your finances will help you see where your spending is necessary or not.

Tuesday 10th

Mercury goes direct today, so you now have a chance to apologise or put something right regarding relationships. You are also now safe to sign contracts or make travel plans that will not be disrupted. Buying something new at this time is also favoured. Go for it.

Wednesday 11th

You are still in the mood to restore harmony to issues that may have arisen during Mercury retrograde. Short trips may be necessary today or a lot of emails and messages. You will feel stuck in your daily routine sector for a couple of weeks and will need to listen to your elders.

Thursday 12th

Deep issues from the past may surface. You will begin to look at why you behave in certain ways and realise that these patterns are not your own but were conditioned by your family. Who are you really?

Friday 13th

You will continue to explore themes around family, mother, secrets and ways in which you are like, or unlike, your family. Digging deep into the roots of the family tree might upset some people, so please be sensitive when you do this. Some things are best kept hidden.

Saturday 14th

There are some nice connections in the heavens today, which mean that your sex life, dream life and energy are all in sync. You would do well to share some quality time with either your loved ones or go on a date with a special person.

Sunday 15th

Mercury is at a critical degree of your relationship sector. There is something bothering you and you need to get it out of your mind and say it. The Moon in your sector of self-expression and creativity can help you do this in a sensitive way.

Monday 16th

As Mercury moves into your sex, death and rebirth sector he has a dreamy edge to him, and you can now freely communicate with partners about your fantasies. You may also be making plans together and sharing the cost of something you have both dreamed of doing. This could be a spiritual retreat.

Tuesday 17th

Expect the unexpected over the next week or so. You could be looking at building an empire or destroying one. This could be related to your current career and standing in the community. Dedicate some time to making subtle changes and not ones that will rock the foundations.

Wednesday 18th

It's another day where you will be thinking about your health, and how your energy can be easily drained by the mundane jobs you have to do. You love to shine and lead, but are your commitments causing your glow to dim a little? Where do you feel small?

Thursday 19th

Today you should be paying some attention to your significant other and key relationships. Compromise is something that does not come easily, but it would do you good to see that the world does not revolve around you. Let others share your light.

Friday 20th

The spring equinox occurs today and balance is the theme. You will feel fired up, enthusiastic and ready to make travel plans. Warrior Mars likes to hear this and is talking to the luck planet Jupiter, who can help add positivity to these plans.

Saturday 21st

Heart and head meet today as Moon and Mercury sit together in your sector of sex, death and rebirth. A good talk with a partner can help you see what changes should be made to help dreams and fantasies become realities. Transform something old into something new.

Sunday 22nd

Saturn moves into your relationship sector and will stay for approximately two-and-a-half years. While here, he will be teaching you a great lesson about how you relate to others, how you are part of a group and how innovative you can be if you want to.

Monday 23rd

Mars and Pluto are now sitting together in your health and duty sector. This pair can tear something down and make it into something new. You will need to figure out what in this area of your life needs to change, or it will be done without your choice.

Tuesday 24th

A New Moon in your travel sector is an excellent opportunity for you to make some plans to conquer new worlds, learn about other cultures and start a new course of learning. Today you should write or draw a vision board of what you would like to do.

Wednesday 25th

Did you make a vision board yesterday? How does it look? Today is another chance to make resolutions, and whatever you decide to do can see you blazing a trail and being a true leader. Don't follow the pack, lead it.

Thursday 26th

You may feel that you are being pulled in all directions. Fear not, as this will soon pass. You should use this opportunity to stand at the centre and look at everything from all angles. Your emotions will be on the edge of erupting at work, so keep them under control.

Friday 27th

Stay in that holding pace from yesterday. Do not make any moves toward certain areas in favour of others. Just keep assessing everything and be a passive observer. The tension is difficult for you, especially at work, but you will get a better idea of the big picture.

Saturday 28th

Venus steps in to help in your career sector, and also begins talks across the boardroom with Jupiter in your duties sector. Venus can sweet-talk the boss and soften any blows if things do not quite go your way. Be as good as gold today.

Sunday 29th

Take the opportunity to enjoy time with friends today. Sharing information, general catch-ups and friendly chatter will help ease the recent tension you have been feeling. You will want to have your partners in crime around and will enjoy being one of the gang.

Monday 3oth

Mars is giving you one last push in your health and duty sector. It is a 'now or never' feeling. Will you run that marathon or won't you? You need to have one last burst of focused energy before applying it to something else.

Tuesday 31st

As Mars joins Saturn the teacher, he receives his next mission – relationships. Mars takes this very well, knowing that his energy and drive will be all about pleasing himself and Venus for the next couple of weeks. Lucky you!

APRIL
. . . .

Wednesday 1st
The Moon in your dreaming sector is making a great
connection with Mercury and Neptune in your sex,
death and rebirth sector. You can talk about dreams and
fantasies easily. You should be able to discuss things that
can possibly be transformed into something sweeter.

Thursday 2nd
Your emotions and feelings will be all about you
today. You could feel quite needy and sensitive, or go
completely the other way and be loud and obnoxious.
Either way, the tendency to want to be number one
surfaces now, so err on the positive side.

Friday 3rd
Venus, the planet of love, moves into your social sector
and adds beauty and harmony to your friendship groups.
You could find yourself dining out more than usual
during this time. People will come together to achieve
balance now and, hopefully, it will involve you.

Saturday 4th

Venus is having a nice chat with Saturn today, who is in
your relationship sector and asking you to think about
the ways you are present for other people. Where are you
part of the pack and where are you a lone wolf? Today the
balance is between social groups and special people.

Sunday 5th

Think about money and check your bank balance.
Is there enough for necessities and a little left over
for fun? As Jupiter and Pluto meet in your health
and duty sector, you could experience a big boost
or a falling out with friends.

Monday 6th

You may be worrying about your finances, which could
cause you some stress. This will not be good for your
health, so maybe practise yoga or calming exercises.
Breathe deeply, be mindful of your thoughts wandering
and return to your problems when you are centred.

Tuesday 7th

You are feeling more balanced, so it would do you good
to check in with friends and family. Small tasks need to
be completed and you may be running a lot of errands.
Be careful of conflict with your significant other.

Wednesday 8th

A Full Moon occurs today in your sector of short trips and communication. It will show where you have been gathering and sharing information. Look out for gossipers as they will be exposed. Issues related to brothers and sisters will come to the fore too. Have you been neglecting them?

Thursday 9th

This could be a volatile day. The Moon in your family sector makes tense connections to Mars in your relationship sector, as well as Uranus in your career sector. Disruption is everywhere, so it's best to lie low and keep away from it all.

Friday 10th

Yesterday's tension is still buzzing around. The emphasis is scattered across many areas, and you feel unable to focus. Nothing can be resolved today, but you can sit back and make mental notes about how you are going to approach this when the mood lifts.

Saturday 11th

Self-expression is easier now that you have sat on a matter. There is a great connection between head and heart, and saying what you mean comes freely. You are energised because you finally feel seen and heard. Words can get you far now.

Sunday 12th

Keep saying what you mean, without hesitation.
The planets are all in favour of you discussing rules,
regulations and what is right or not. You can make plans
and commitments now, both to yourself and to other
people or groups. You might learn something that is to
your advantage.

Monday 13th

The daily grind is keeping you sane right now.
Emotionally, you just want to get through the day, go
to the gym, eat a nice dinner and have some 'me' time.
Following a routine will benefit you and keep you away
from anything that could cause stress.

Tuesday 14th

You can clearly see something that needs to change. It
could be a task you do every day, certain eating habits
or even your exercise regime. You will feel stubborn
about having to make this shift and sit on it for a while.
You do not need to change now, however, just simply
think about it.

Wednesday 15th

Are you feeling blocked? You may want to show up and show off but something external or even internal is preventing that from happening. This could be a good thing because you need to consider how you are coming across to others. Leader or dictator?

Thursday 16th

Your mood turns towards relationships again and, in particular, your significant other. If you are single, you may find that this makes you look inward to your shadow side. Give your shadow some love. It is there to be nurtured, so make friends with it today.

Friday 17th

Today you will be thinking about secrets, taboo subjects and how in control you are. You may want to go deep and seek out treasure from a very dark place. Be brave enough to face the darkness and see what light is hidden there.

Saturday 18th

Talking to your social group about foreign lands and cultures creates a yearning to travel. Listening to stories about your friends' experiences makes you want to research and mark a few places on the map. Where does your heart want to go? What would you like to discover?

Sunday 19th

The Sun moves into your career sector and brings with it a new energy and drive. You could now be talking about moving your career overseas or the possibility of trips connected with business. Will this satisfy your urge to travel? Do all your research first.

Monday 20th

Still thinking about travel and exploration? You dream of the future and where you see yourself in two, five or ten years' time. You want to start something new and exciting, maybe learn a foreign language even. Now is a good time to make plans.

Tuesday 21st

Love and romance are uncomplicated today and flow easily. Your mood makes relating easy and pleasant. However, you may now be finding reasons not to move forwards with career plans or there may be rules enforced on you. Look for all the pros and cons and weigh it all up.

Wednesday 22nd

Balancing your social life with your love life is not so tricky now. You may meet someone in your social group who you click with, and this could turn into something romantic. Do not try finding reasons why this is not a good idea before even trying it.

Thursday 23rd

A New Moon in your career sector gives you a golden opportunity to consider how you lead and how you want to advance. You can build solid foundations to ensure that every step up the ladder is a step towards security. Commitment and dedication are needed now.

Friday 24th

Continue to write your New Moon aspirations. What would you like to be remembered for? Do you have a career goal that requires a good strategy? Is there something completely new that you want to start?

Saturday 25th

Today you will be thinking about influence and control. Mercury (thinking and talking) faces Pluto (power), and this can be an uncomfortable meeting of tactic talks. The Moon in your social circle wants you to go and have fun with friends and let off some steam.

Sunday 26th

Yesterday's tactic talks were because Pluto is now retrograde. This will happen completely in your duties and health sector, and you will have to review where your power is being drained or where you are giving it away. Watch out for any exposures at work because something could flare up.

Monday 27th

The Moon in your dreams sector makes you want to
switch off and retreat. Today is a day for comfort foods
and pillow forts. Watching an old favourite movie
can help you feel nurtured and satisfied. Meanwhile,
workaholic Mercury has entered your career sector and
is ready to network.

Tuesday 28th

You will feel isolated today, unless retreat is self-
inflicted. Stay away from anything like alcohol or bad TV,
and instead indulge in daydreaming about your perfect
future. What do you need to feel good about yourself?
Consider a scenario where this is ample.

Wednesday 29th

Staying with the theme of the future, you may feel
somewhat restricted by new plans. You may become
overwhelmed and feel unable to change anything yet.
Think big, dream big and lucky Jupiter will help you to
see some answers.

Thursday 30th

The Moon pays its monthly visit to your sign. You may
have been indulging yourself lately, so now is the time
to get out from under your duvet and shine. Arriving
like a newborn can lift you out of retreat and back into
the world.

MAY

. . . .

Friday 1st

Mercury has only just popped into your career sector
and already he has plenty to say. He is sitting right on
top of Uranus, so expect the unexpected. A revolution
or strike is on the cards. You will want to take action today.

Saturday 2nd

Your mind turns towards money matters, and you
are wondering if you could, or should, splash out on
something. You feel rebellious, but a little devil, or angel,
on your shoulder asks you to consider all options. Is it
going to make you feel better?

Sunday 3rd

You feel fired up by Mercury's words, and they go deep
into your heart. You will still be feeling the twitch
of something radical and exciting happening in the
workplace. Something is about to change – for good or
bad. Make the change or be part of it.

Monday 4th

Lots of small tasks and catching up with family members will make you feel balanced today. Mercury has gone AWOL, and so whatever trouble he stirred up is now left for everyone else to clean up. Just do what needs doing today.

Tuesday 5th

Where is Mercury when you need him? There is a shift in thinking today, and it doesn't just involve you. There will be a general feeling of collecting and sharing information, platonic love and short travel. You will feel this most in your social sector.

Wednesday 6th

You could be digging up the family tree again today. Family history is fascinating, and you want to know all that there is to know about several generations. Which of your traits have you inherited and from whom? Can you relate to your genealogy or does it repulse you?

Thursday 7th

While you are digging up your roots, a Full Moon illuminates something shiny in the corner. Dare you investigate it? Secrets, lies and espionage are all waiting to be exposed today, but be careful as you may raise some demons too. Prepare to face dark elements. You must take responsibility for this now.

Friday 8th

Do you wish to explore any further today? Maybe you should turn your attention to foreign travel and how this could grow your soul and touch your heart. You can express yourself freely now, and will be admired for doing so. You want to know what more is out there.

Saturday 9th

Mercury is still trying to shake things up in your career sector. He is urging you to do your research and gather all the information about something before presenting it. Pluto is telling Mercury that he must instigate change. What can you do?

Sunday 10th

You have a lucky streak in your career today. What is it that you want to present to those in charge next week? This could be a day where you realise the best ways to be heard and win others round to your way of thinking.

Monday 11th

That great teacher Saturn goes retrograde today. He had only just dipped his toe in your relationship sector but now returns to teach you something about health and duty. Was there something in this area that you did not manage to complete or bring to fruition?

Tuesday 12th

Mercury has left your career sector and is now dancing around with your friends and social groups. However, you must remember to keep your friends close and your enemies closer. Use Mercury well and have some fun.

Wednesday 13th

Venus will begin retracing her steps in your social sector today. Things will not be easy for the next forty days with issues arising around love, money and friends. It is best to separate these issues before they become entangled and cause trouble.

Thursday 14th

Take care with your significant other now or try dancing with your shadow side. The Moon is in your opposite sign and this is about relationships or your inner demons. With Venus now retrograde, it is better to stay home alone and do your inner work than to hurt someone else.

Friday 15th

Jupiter, the planet of luck and joy, joins the retrograde party, becoming another character sitting in your sector of health and duty. This is the theme for you this year, and there are important issues that these retrogrades will bring to light.

Saturday 16th

Your mood and dreams are not in synch today. Venus retrograde in your social sector is making her first uneasy connection to the Moon, which is currently in your area that deals with sex, transformation and shared finances. Dealing with others today could be problematic, be considerate and careful.

Sunday 17th

You may get a glimpse of what needs to change today. This will be in your health and duty sector. It could just be mundane daily activities but whatever it is, the overhaul will be big. If you do not take action then it will be taken for you, and that will not be easy. Take the initiative and feel the benefits.

Monday 18th

Communication with friends is featured today. Some socialising or just chatting online with your favourite people can be just what is needed. You are willing and able to listen to the feelings of others and to share your own.

Tuesday 19th

Yesterday's theme of easy-going conversation extends to loved ones today. You can express your heartfelt desires and allow yourself some little luxuries. Pamper yourself with delicious food or a scented bath, things which make you feel good. You may even get a nice surprise coming your way.

Wednesday 20th

As the Moon moves into your career sector, the Sun will move into your social sector. There is nothing you like more than being in the limelight, so the next month could be fun-filled and friendly. You will be thinking again about leadership and how you can stand out in your field.

Thursday 21st

You may be feeling moody or fed up at work today. If that's the case, try to leave your emotions outside and maintain a professional air so as not to cause an atmosphere or upset colleagues. Luckily, this is all down to a Moon phase so it will pass quickly. When it's over, you can return happily to the job of getting out there with your tribe.

Friday 22nd

Today brings a New Moon in your social sector. You can show fresh intentions or sow seeds about how you would like to pursue new friendships or projects. Is there anything that you have been itching to do that may be a bit risky? Today is the day – seize the opportunity and give it a go!

Saturday 23rd

Actions, tempers and cross words may occur today. You are feeling touchy and want to do something about it, but your body and emotions are just not working together. Don't force it, this could be a day to lie low.

Sunday 24th

You could be triggered by feelings about your mother or the home in which you were brought up. Your own parenting could also be a theme. This could come as a surprise and stir feelings that have been buried deeply. You could also have fond memories.

Monday 25th

Today you are at risk of retreating inwards and self-medicating on junk food, alcohol or trashy TV. You may not want to come out and play. The best thing to do is compromise with wholesome comfort food and a good box set.

Tuesday 26th

The gloomy mood continues and you become quite fatalistic. You perceive your world as tumbling down around you. This is just the necessary change that you will grow from, and it will transform into something better. Smile and look on the sunny side as the Sun, your ruler, would do.

Wednesday 27th

The Moon now comes into your sign, which means your self-indulgent mood will continue. You will be affronted when people do not pay you enough attention. Flip this over and be the star of your own show.

Thursday 28th

Mercury has very quickly now entered your dreaming sector, so thinking and communicating may become foggy. Ideas will go as quickly as they come, and you will not be able to grasp anything. Try keeping a dream diary during this time, as that may make more sense than your waking thoughts.

Friday 29th

You need to come back down to earth! Try fixing your mind on something solid, such as your money and possessions. You could rearrange your home or dream about new styles and fashions. Having nice things around you is important now.

Saturday 30th

Today you could be thinking about what it is around you and in your home that makes you feel good. You might also think the opposite. A bit of feng shui will not go amiss today. Rededicate yourself and home to a healthy lifestyle.

Sunday 31st

Today is another one of those days where small tasks need to be completed. Balance your finances, check in with loved ones and tick off your list of chores. You may find yourself running around a lot but at the end of the day, you will have satisfaction.

JUNE
....

Monday 1st
Today you may feel that things are getting you down.
You could be tired and drained, and feel that you are
doing too much for other people and not taking care of
yourself. You feel edgy and irritable. Take time out and
do something just for you.

Tuesday 2nd
Family affairs are occupying your mind, and you will feel
any slight tension deeply. Venus and Mars are clashing,
so there will be obstructions in your love life and any
relating matters with others. This is a tense day where
you struggle to get what you want.

Wednesday 3rd
There is a bipolar theme to today's energy. You will be
open to talking about deep feelings but you must be
prepared for arguments and battles of will. You feel that
you are not being seen or heard, which will make you
wish you hadn't opened up to someone.

Thursday 4th

You might feel like ending something today. Mars, the planet of direct, action is in your area of sex, death and rebirth. Venus retrograde asks you to consider what you value, and this could mean that you assess your relationships. You may feel that you are better off by yourself.

Friday 5th

A Full Moon in your self-expression area is a wonderful opportunity to be yourself and go all out to get your needs met. However, this could also make you very selfish, and you may leave people behind in your shadow. Something could show up unexpectedly and hurt you.

Saturday 6th

You turn towards mundane routines today. You will ignore any outside aggravations and just move along with your head down. You do not want to cause or be involved in any more upset. Attend only to what is necessary. Everything else can wait.

Sunday 7th

Turn the phone off and have a day to yourself.
Things have been pretty tense lately, so you would
be best keeping your blood pressure down by doing
uninteresting things. The time will come for you to act
again, but it is not today.

Monday 8th

You are feeling the need to make big changes and get
your life back in your control. Being as quiet as you have
been for the last few days does not suit you, but it was
necessary. There could be power struggles, so please be
careful and show compassion where needed.

Tuesday 9th

Your partner or close family and friends will require
attention today. This will be hard for you if you are still
holding a grudge against someone. You will feel restricted
by others and will want to be the only lion in your pride.
Take care that your shadow side does not surface.

Wednesday 10th

You will receive some insight into how your relationships function today, and you will see where you have been deluding yourself or someone else has deceived you. Rose-tinted glasses come off and you are left reeling. Take time to think before reacting.

Thursday 11th

You would do yourself a favour to look at any financial obligations that you share with someone else. Where can you possibly cut back or cut out? Relationships are still on your mind, and you must now look at where you have commitments with another person that can be rearranged.

Friday 12th

Relationships are still bothering you. Do certain ones make you feel undervalued and as if your own needs are not met? How might you communicate this in a way that does not cause an argument? Be a gentle lion now.

Saturday 13th

The Moon meets both Mars and Neptune in your sex sector today. Mars usually understands what Venus wants, but she is evaluating things privately before re-emerging. Neptune can make things surreal and unclear. Wait until the Moon passes and you will be better equipped to see the real picture.

Sunday 14th

You feel more energised today, and you'll want to make plans for holidays to get away from the recent tension. You will be dreaming of places you would like to visit and working these into future plans. You are called to go off on your own now.

Monday 15th

You may start to research the holiday destinations you are yearning to visit. Gather information and watch films about the places that are calling you. Fill your head with these dreams. If nothing else, they are a harmless retreat from the daily grind that you can enjoy alone.

Tuesday 16th

You feel a little more balanced today. Your emotional and physical states are in sync, and you can express yourself with ease. You will be centred on your career for now, and able to think up new ways to advance in your chosen field.

Wednesday 17th

Saturn, the teacher, returns to your daily routine sector. What is his lesson here for you? When a planet returns to the last degrees of a sign, it is asking you what unfinished business you have in this area. He could also be asking you to remember something that you have forgotten.

Thursday 18th

Mercury starts another retrograde period today, and he will be doing this in your dreams area. This is also the space where you can drift off alone, enjoy solitude and explore spiritual ventures. You may need to get some facts right now.

Friday 19th

Remember not to make too many new commitments when Mercury is retrograde, as they will be unlikely to come to anything. Now is the time to review the recent past. Family, especially mothers, could be highlighted today and once more power issues will come to the surface.

Saturday 20th

Aggression could get out of hand today. Mars is talking to Jupiter, who just makes everything bigger. Direct words and actions are best kept to yourself now as they could end up in a volatile mess. Something is brewing and coming to a head, so try to remain calm.

Sunday 21st

Today the summer solstice also has a solar eclipse. As the Sun is your ruler, this day usually revitalises you. However, the Moon will overshadow the Sun, putting a spanner in the works. Something big is about to take place, so get out of the way!

Monday 22nd

Yesterday's solar eclipse has produced some strange energy, and you feel like having a day under the duvet with comfort foods. Retreat is fine if you are avoiding problems that do not concern you, but do not be a cowardly lion if they are your problems. Face them head-on.

Tuesday 23rd

The Moon enters your sign, and you know that this means you will want to have your needs met or be the centre of attention. If you are still under the blankets and being good to yourself like yesterday, then carry on as you are.

Wednesday 24th

Neptune, the planet that makes things foggy and helps us dream, has now gone retrograde. He could put another blanket on you, which may be comforting. There is also a danger today of self-medicating with alcohol or bad food in order to switch off from everything.

Thursday 25th

There is a saving grace today. Venus is direct again and your love life and money can receive a lift. There may be some lingering issues to deal with, but the worst is over for now. You can stop feeling sorry for yourself and be more proactive.

Friday 26th

You could be looking at a crossroads today. Mars, in your sex, death and rebirth sector, is feeling pulled between the past and future. Something you have let go of recently still has a grip on you. Cut the cords and move on.

Saturday 27th

You are feeling the effects of Mars strongly now. The Moon is opposite him, and you have a battle raging in your heart. Mars is at the last degree of Pisces, and is urging you to end something before moving forward.

Sunday 28th

Mars moves into his own sign today, and he wants you to make big plans. Exercise and expansion are the keywords for this time, but you must take care not to let the hot-headed warrior take over. Determination with compassion is what you need now.

Monday 29th

Has Mars come to a halt already? This is only a minor hiccup as the Moon passes all those planets in your daily routine sector. Keep going with your new adventure and travel plans, and resist the urge to procrastinate or sabotage yourself.

Tuesday 30th

Big changes are happening. Very big and very deep. There is a chance that nothing will ever be the same. If you do not want to be unwillingly swept away, you must lead the change. Otherwise, the universe will do it for you.

JULY

. . . .

Wednesday 1st

As July opens, Saturn is right at the beginning of your
relationship sector, and is covering some old ground
for you to work on. Mercury has nothing to say, so take
this opportunity to listen instead. He is in your sex,
death and rebirth sector, so pay close attention to your
inner voice.

Thursday 2nd

The Moon moves into your creative sector. This could
be a good time to listen to your dreams and continue
the theme from Mercury. What are your dream symbols
telling you? Could you put them down on paper and get
an artistic viewpoint?

Friday 3rd

Saturn is now moving backwards in your health and
duty sector. While here, he wants you to take a good look
at your own boundaries and those of other people. Are
you spending lots of time selflessly helping others? Are
you being taken for granted?

Saturday 4th

Today your emotions are full of ifs, buts and cannots. You feel a heavy restriction on steps you want to take regarding your health and exercise routines. This is another chance to look at where your energy goes, and what you can do about it.

Sunday 5th

Today's Full Moon and lunar eclipse will show you how far you are willing to go to achieve your goals. Look back at something you have strived for. Did you make it? Did you get to the top? What projects failed to come to completion? You have a chance to put all of it right now.

Monday 6th

Today is a great day for socialising as the Moon connects with Venus, who is currently dancing around your friendship sector. The Moon herself is concerned with your one-to-one relationships, so think of a way to combine your lover and your friends.

Tuesday 7th

Is there something you have planned with a social group that could be an outing for all? This is a favourable day for any activities that are unusual and exciting. This could also take the form of protests and activism, helping you feel truly part of your tribe.

Wednesday 8th

Your emotions can be deep and intense today. You need to watch out for accidents and arguments, because Mars and Mercury are not playing nicely. This will affect you in adventure and travel and also relationships. Remember that Mercury is still retrograde and can wreak havoc.

Thursday 9th

Today, you will need to analyse the difference between wants and needs. Your wants are concerned with your friendship groups, and your needs seem to lie with a special person. Consider what is really necessary, what is true and what is just something that you desire.

Friday 10th

You feel conflicted today between spending time with a partner and having casual fun with friends. Both are great options, but which will serve you best overall? Do not swap long-term for short-term gains. Be wise.

Saturday 11th

Today you will feel more outgoing and adventurous, and return to dreaming about far-flung places. You may even be thinking about a new course of study, possibly learning a new language or researching a different culture to your own. Dining out at an exotic restaurant also appeals.

Sunday 12th

Mercury goes direct today, so you can breathe again!
You must go and apologise for any upset caused in the
last three weeks. You feel like a fog is lifting and can see
more clearly. Now you can think about that new contract
or commitment.

Monday 13th

As the Moon enters your career sector, you will be
looking at how to advance or climb the corporate ladder
– perhaps in a different way to one you had previously
thought about. Mercury's forward motion can help these
dreams come true now.

Tuesday 14th

With regards to work and career, there could be some
surprises in store. You could shock yourself by your
emotional response to something that is said. Try not to
take things the wrong way. Instead, pause for thought
and take one step at a time.

Wednesday 15th

Power struggles at work can weigh you down today.
Something could be exposed that was once undercover,
and it may cause an upset. Like yesterday, you need to
keep yourself under control and just watch the whole
scenario play out without getting involved. If this is your
issue, tread carefully.

Thursday 16th

Time to get out and about with friends. You will want to let off some steam, and your tribe will be supportive and encouraging. Enjoy swapping stories, telling jokes and venting with social or online groups.

Friday 17th

You seem to be able to get everything you want today, so feel free to wish for your heart's desire. Friends adore you and are eager to please. This is not surprising, because when you are happy you are the life and soul of the party.

Saturday 18th

The family in which you were brought up plays a significant role today. You could find yourself daydreaming about your childhood and wondering about your own parenting role. You want to feel nurtured and safe, if only in your thoughts.

Sunday 19th

The Moon meets Mercury today in your dreaming sector. What does your heart want to tell your head and vice versa? Give both equal space, otherwise the conversation will be one-sided and not get anywhere. Practise active listening.

Monday 20th

The New Moon will give you a chance to make mini resolutions regarding family issues. This is a time of new beginnings, yet it is also about endings. There may be family members that you would prefer to distance yourself from, and you will be thinking about personal boundaries.

Tuesday 21st

This is an odd time for you as the Moon enters your sign. You will behave in two very different ways. You might be the sunshine of everyone's life or the party pooper who throws a tantrum. The choice is yours.

Wednesday 22nd

Today the Sun returns to your sign, so this is your birthday month. You will feel energised over the next few weeks, and have a great party as only you know how. Time to put your glad rags on and be the star of your own show.

Thursday 23rd

Words might come out of your mouth today and you will have no idea where they came from. Just take care that they are not hurtful. You could surprise yourself and friends with some stand-up comedy. Keep an eye on finances, and spend only what is necessary.

Friday 24th

If you have the feeling that you are throwing money away or it is going down the drain, then you need to look for reasons why this might be. Balance the books and make sure you know where your money is going every month. If someone owes you money, perhaps a gentle reminder might be in order.

Saturday 25th

Balancing is the name of the game today. You could be splitting your time between friends, family and urgent chores. Yet this is an easy day where you will get a lot done if you stay on task and make sure everyone is happy. Check in with some phone calls and catch up with those closest to you.

Sunday 26th

Talkative Mercury may be in your head today, and you will not be able to shift him. You will have a heart versus head battle, but it is not serious. This is just one of those days where a thought is on loop and you cannot get rid of it. Don't pay it too much attention and things will quickly settle down again.

Monday 27th

This is not an easy day. It will be rather intense as there are many planets involved in a stand-off. The themes for you are about friendships versus lovers, and dreams versus actions. How are you going to play this one? Stay home.

Tuesday 28th

You will want to get out, stay out and have a great time. This might not be easy though, as Lady Luck is not on your side today and you are faced with a brick wall at every turn. Your dreams are perhaps too large and unrealistic.

Wednesday 29th

You still have the urge to go out and about today, and the energy is more amenable. You can be creative, and self-expression will come easily. It's a lovely day with the sun shining in the direction of where you want to go.

Thursday 30th

Listen out for lies and deceit, as you may uncover some secrets or untruths. On the other hand, your legendary storytelling abilities may put you in the spotlight. Make sure you are not the one telling the tall tales.

Friday 31st

A humdrum day where you just get on with chores. Routine things sustain you and do not cause you any trouble. Enjoy uncomplicated days like these because they do not come around very often. Please also check in with your health and ensure that all is well.

AUGUST

. . . .

Saturday 1st
Mercury is in your dreaming sector, and is still trying to
make your plans, dreams and visions a reality. The seeds
of these dreams need to be held onto for just a little
while longer before you can plant them. Mind chatter
will be at a high level today.

Sunday 2nd
The Moon's influence may show up your shadow side
in important relationships today. Expect something to
erupt out of nowhere. Double-check to see if this is
coming from inside of you or if it is issues belonging to
the other person.

Monday 3rd
A Full Moon in your opposite sign of Aquarius
illuminates your shadow in all its darkest glory. There
may be some revelations about the deepest parts of you
or your relationships. These are matters that need to be
brought to the surface and healed. Deal with them.

Tuesday 4th

Energetic Mars wants you to go and get what you want today. Self-expression can be rather direct and cutting, and this may be a day when things get blown out of proportion if you are not careful. Curb the need to always be right.

Wednesday 5th

Today you may feel moody and brood over things that you want and cannot have. You feel the need to end something to make room for the new. Mercury enters your sign, so there is a lot going on in your head now. Time to plant those seeds.

Thursday 6th

Your yearning for change makes you look at love and money today. You will factor these into your dreams and wonder how to combine both to move forwards. Friends and social groups may give you the impetus and ideas on how to do this.

Friday 7th

Venus now enters your dream sector, and you will find that the next couple of weeks can be quite dreamy and positive. Venus rules love, beauty and harmony, so your dreams may be painted in beautiful colours. She will also make you think about family issues.

Saturday 8th

Your mood will wander between family issues and blazing a trail on your own. You have a sense of adventure, and a hero's quest starts to form in your mind. You will start to research journeys and they could be inner or outer ones.

Sunday 9th

What is preventing you from realising and developing your plans? In what areas would you like to grow? You may feel some resistance from your everyday duties and obligations, and resent that these seem to be holding you back. You have free will, so use it.

Monday 10th

Your career takes centre stage today, and you will feel the urge to stir something up. Your restlessness may result in some mistakes, but play your cards right and anything you agitate can work in your favour. Be a rebel with a cause.

Tuesday 11th

Heart and head are in battle today, and neither of them are budging. When you have a day like this, it is best to be the passive observer and see just what it is both sides want. Try to listen and gain balance.

Wednesday 12th

Have a day with friends today. Your social group or tribe are the ones who know you best and value you the most. You will gain much by being a social butterfly and networking with people of the same frame of mind as you.

Thursday 13th

Who is in control? Power struggles and issue relating to temper, quarrels and aggression will arise today. You want to win and leave the loser far behind you, but choose your battles wisely. Conquest will not always bring personal satisfaction.

Friday 14th

The power struggles continue today, and you find that they are between what you want to do and what you have to do. Duties make you feel stuck, while all you want to do is run away to a new country and make your mark. Vigorous exercise will help relieve this tension.

Saturday 15th

The mood lifts and you are now much more positive about realising your dreams and plans. The Moon is making nice connections to Venus in your dream sector, while Mars is given the go-ahead in your travel sector by an easy connection with the Sun.

Sunday 16th

Yesterday's nice vibes quickly turn once again to blockages and restrictions. These will soon pass as it is the effect of the Moon, and she moves on quickly. The best thing to do is persist and not pay too much attention.

Monday 17th

The Moon has arrived in your sign, so you can focus on yourself. You will feel either energised or moody. You may swing between the golden child and outright show-off. Tantrums will come easily, so be your best self and show people a bright, shiny side.

Tuesday 18th

A New Moon is in your sign today, and this is your golden ticket to start a new venture where you can truly be yourself. Think upon your divine purpose in this life and go for it. Remember those seeds you planted and nurture them well.

Wednesday 19th

You will be thinking about putting everything in order. A good clear out and organisation of your home, finances and possessions is the first step to realising the goals you have set for yourself under yesterday's New Moon. Declutter your life.

Thursday 20th

Mercury joins the ongoing clean-up party, and is great at delegating tasks. He will help you get the job done and to do it methodically. With him as your chairman, you will get to the bottom of everything and leave nothing undone.

Friday 21st

You might feel distracted today, and have to attend to matters that are not your own. Emails, text messages and phone calls can be a help or a hindrance. Choose the important things and let the others go for now. File them for later.

Saturday 22nd

The Sun is leaving your sign, which means the focus is still going to be on your money and possessions. You must pay attention to the small details and ensure that all bases are covered. Look after your health now, too. Don't overdo it.

Sunday 23rd

Intense emotions come now. Although this is just a Moon phase, it is a useful time to do some inner work. If something is bothering you, try to get to the bottom of it. Family issues can surface but these also have gold hidden in them.

Monday 24th

There is tension around you today. Is it coming from outside or inside? You may feel like an authority figure has sent you to the naughty step, and you will want to throw a tantrum in protest. Stamping your feet will not do you any good, so sit tight and try to find the lesson.

Tuesday 25th

Your mood lifts, and you feel all fired up and ready to go places. Self-expression comes easily now and you can be creative and playful. This is the perfect time to indulge your inner child, so get out the crayons and make some messy art. Anything will do, as long as it expresses your individuality.

Wednesday 26th

Keep playing, get out there and be the hero in your own adventure story. You have the energy of a true pioneer right now, so use it wisely and transform it into something you can dream about. You are the zodiac's greatest performer. Give the world a show.

Thursday 27th

It's back to the daily grind. You must review your health and maybe make a check-up appointment. Duties can distract you, but they will also keep you in a peaceful mood as nothing unusual will happen at this time. Your dreams and visions will receive a positive boost.

Friday 28th

Pleasant surprises can come your way now. Your career is highlighted but this could also be about your home and your finances. If you keep your eyes open there may be some doors opening for you. Avoid any negative people and keep the cheery mood going.

Saturday 29th

There are a lot of connections happening in the sky today. You may feel a small conflict between your needs and your wants. You will also come up against the usual things that you feel restrict your growth. Stop with the self-sabotage and move beyond it.

Sunday 30th

Pay your loved one a little attention today. There is a chance that your shadow side can come out, and unrealistic ideals will surface. Be kind and avoid the rose-tinted glasses or the urge to control. See things for what they are.

Monday 31st

You are in the mood to be forceful and direct today but this will be in the nicest possible way. You can practise the art of being a spiritual warrior, and get things done without aggression or coercion. This is a very valuable lesson.

SEPTEMBER

....

Tuesday 1st

As a dreamy Moon enters your area that deals with secrets and intensity, you can expect to be swimming in oceans beyond your imagination. Take note of all that you find there, and it may just be possible to make those dreams a reality.

Wednesday 2nd

Today's Full Moon can highlight all that you desire and if your needs are being met. Are you where you are supposed to be? You may feel uprooted or cast adrift and this can be very unsettling. Stay grounded and keep away from the edge.

Thursday 3rd

The dreamy mood has passed and you feel more action-orientated today, however you will need to check in with your health as you could still be feeling fuzzy. Clear the fog and set some goals, especially for travel and exploration.

Friday 4th

Venus and Mars are quarrelling today, so you may find that action and dreaming are out of sync. Venus is in the sign of the mother, which may mean that female authority figures feature in these upsets too. All you can do is listen.

Saturday 5th

Communication will be on your mind now. You will be listening to many points of view and trying to find a balance upon which you can base new research. You may find that you are called on to be a mediator in family disputes, and will be asked for words of wisdom.

Sunday 6th

Your mood is preoccupied with career. This is by no means a bad thing, as you will become dedicated to tasks in the hopes of a reward. Luckily, Venus has moved into your sign and she is ready to give treats where deserved.

Monday 7th

You can be the genius today or you can be the upstart. At work, people will look to you for your innovative ways of solving problems, but try not to think too much outside the box and unwittingly alienate yourself. Colleagues need you and you need them.

Tuesday 8th

Leisure time with friends will be good for you today. You can have an easy time with all those who are still listening to your ideas. Keeping things real and being a social butterfly is the best course of action.

Wednesday 9th

The Sun is talking to Jupiter, and the Moon is shopping with Venus. You can spoil yourself a little but be warned, you will have the tendency to overspend and regret it later. Be modest if you can, although you are not always known for your modesty!

Thursday 10th

Mars goes retrograde today in your travel sector. Just as you thought all that forward marching you have been doing is about to come to something, you now realise that you have to march backwards and amend some details. Going back over old ground will not do you any harm.

Friday 11th

The Moon enters your area of hopes and dreams, but the Sun is directly opposing the dreaming planet Neptune. This means that you will have the ability to see through anything that can usually dazzle you with brilliance. Fog clears and rose-tinted glasses can come off.

Saturday 12th

Today can have a feeling of rigidity, but only if you kept on yesterday's rose-tinted glasses. You want to feel nurtured and cared for, but feel that quite the opposite is happening. You must learn to look after number one, and not ask others to do it.

Sunday 13th

Actions and emotions are difficult to reconcile today. You are feeling moody and need all eyes on you. Jupiter has now resumed a forwards motion in your health and duty sector, so expect things to get an uplift in that area now. Practise self-love, not self-indulgence.

Monday 14th

The Moon and Venus are sitting in the same spot in your area of self now. This can make you feel confident and capable. Try not to fall on the negative side and become narcissistic. Instead, use this beautiful energy to show off your true essence.

Tuesday 15th

Are you in the mood for a makeover? You might be considering cutting your hair or buying a whole new wardrobe. However, think hard before you make any radical changes to your look. The time is not favourable and you will regret it.

Wednesday 16th

Spending frivolously on outrageous items that you will never use is not recommended. You can fulfil that urge by doing something creative instead. Make something for the home and be proud of what you have achieved. You have the capacity to be quite creative.

Thursday 17th

A New Moon this morning in your money sector is a good opportunity to plant seeds, and make affirmations regarding health, money and the little luxuries you enjoy. Your conscience might think that this is a selfish wish, but wishing for 'enough' cannot be a bad thing.

Friday 18th

Striving for balance today between chores and the demands of others can cause you to make problems seem bigger than they are. Plod on through the day getting things done, and what seemed like a mountain will soon look like a molehill.

Saturday 19th

Today you may feel angry and irritable for an unknown reason. It may be that family issues are surfacing that are not really your problem. Take care to step aside and look at where the real root of the problem lies. Don't be controlling.

Sunday 20th

Sudden outbursts are forecast. Again, the family around you seem to be at the centre of it, and you will need to be the mediator and not the agitator. Fits of rage and aggression are likely now, so stay calm and look at things from all possible angles.

Monday 21st

You want to have your say today, so now is your chance. You have the passion to express your own needs, as well as the energy and drive required. Do so in a way that demonstrates your excellent leadership qualities to make your point well.

Tuesday 22nd

The Sun shifts into your area of communication, and once more you are called upon to use your leadership and mediator skills. You may find yourself in the position of being judge and jury in something that has been long-standing in your close friendships.

Wednesday 23rd

Today, an authority figure is going to challenge and confront you with new lessons that you need to learn. These will come from your daily routine, and will ask you to solve problems and maybe change your perspective on an ongoing issue.

Thursday 24th

You need to take a back seat and relax. The recent tension has not been good for your health, and you may be experiencing headaches. Let somebody else do the talking and sorting while you take time to recharge.

Friday 25th

Another quiet day is needed. You feel pulled by your day-to-day activities, but they could be the very distraction you need. Only do what is necessary and leave the rest for another day. You just do not have the energy to deal with it all.

Saturday 26th

Being in the company of a lover, partner or other special person in your life will be good for you. The Moon in your opposite sign can make you needy, but it can also help create a successful day with meaningful connections. Share quality time with someone.

Sunday 27th

Over the next couple of weeks, you will find that secrets and lies are uncovered in your family sector. Family members may tell you things in confidence, and you will be once again called upon to act as a witness or judge. Be discreet.

Monday 28th

Sex and lies will be an ongoing theme for a couple of weeks. Right now the Moon has entered the deepest, darkest part of your chart. It will not be there for more than a couple of days, but at this time be a detective and see what you can uncover.

Tuesday 29th

Venus and Mars, the celestial lovers, are on a friendly date today, so you will notice that recent upsets are calming down and peace can be restored. Saturn also goes direct in your health and duty sector, so you may now think about what lessons you have learnt in this area over the last months.

Wednesday 30th

Today will feel lighter in many respects except for one. Your urge to explore something new is still being halted for now. This is the time to review any travel plans and make any amendments. Saturn, the teacher, wants Mars to listen to tactic talks before progressing.

OCTOBER

. . . .

Thursday 1st

October starts with a Full Moon in your travel sector. What is being highlighted now are seeds you may have planted back in March. Plans to explore new lands are opening up. You have been given the green light.

Friday 2nd

Venus has now entered a great part of your chart. She is sat in the sector that deals with money, beauty, harmony and value, bringing you much good fortune. She will be there for the whole of the month, so make the most of it.

Saturday 3rd

You have a lovely aspect shining on you from above. Venus is in harmony with the Moon, so your wants and needs are balanced. The Moon is accentuating your need for beauty, allowing you to assess what you value most.

Sunday 4th

You may feel conflicted today. After revelling in the recent easy days, you now have a moment of anxiety. Your mind is making up excuses not to value material things and wants you to find worth in deep, spiritual activities. You can do both.

Monday 5th

Pluto, the Lord of Power and Control, joins the other big planets in your health and duty sector and goes direct. You will begin to feel more control over your daily routine, and any health issues may get some reprieve now. You feel more satisfaction in the nine to five.

Tuesday 6th

A great day for socialising. Get out there and entertain friends. Everyone knows you can put on a show or great dinner, so be that person today. Hosting a get-together or attending one will give you equal pleasure.

Wednesday 7th

Be careful what you say today. Mercury is opposing Uranus, the planet of shocks and surprises, and that could lead to trouble in your family or career. Just be mindful to think before you speak, otherwise you could hurt someone close to you. Alternatively, it could be you on the receiving end.

Thursday 8th

Today is one of those days where retreat, solitude or simply being quiet is recommended. Enjoy the comfort foods you liked as a child and watch a good box set. Switch off and enjoy a little fantasy. Have a comfortable day in your pyjamas.

Friday 9th

You are still enjoying some downtime and eating ice cream straight from the tub, yet you also have the desire to make a change. Keep it simple, such as rearranging your living space. Mars, who helps us move, is at odds with Pluto, so overhauling anything that is complicated could prove difficult.

Saturday 10th

All systems have been recharged and you are feeling motivated again. Your emotional needs are not entirely synched with your commitments, but you can still sail through the day easily. Some pleasant surprises or gifts could come your way. Enjoy the small things.

Sunday 11th

Oh dear, you are back to a day where things may not go so well. The Moon is in your sign, but it is also making some bad connections to Uranus and Mercury. It is another day where you will need to curb the urge to say something potentially outrageous or hurtful.

Monday 12th

A day of contemplation today. You will be looking back at where you have been, as well as forwards to where you would like to go. What skills can you take into the future, and what definitely needs to be left behind? Do nothing except consider this.

Tuesday 13th
Tempers could flare today. There is heightened tension because the Sun is shining right on Mars in your travel sector. Mars is still retrograde and not getting where he wants to go, so the best plan is to try and see what his lesson is.

Wednesday 14th
Mercury retrograde warning! A big part of yesterday's tension was a preview for the next couple of weeks. Mercury has been thinking about, talking about and listening to everyone's secrets and he may just be ready to reveal all. Keep your counsel until it is all over.

Thursday 15th
You could find yourself involved in a power struggle today. You do what is expected of you, but someone may push for more. Stand your ground. You give enough of yourself to certain people and that is commendable. Any more would be exhausting.

Friday 16th
A New Moon in your area of short journeys and communication is a chance to make mini resolutions and plant seeds. This one is in Libra, and asks you to consider where you end and another begins. Aim for harmony and balance in how you speak to others and honour their boundaries.

Saturday 17th

Your family sector is in the spotlight today. Saying what is on your mind and in your heart feels imperative. This could be upsetting, but it's necessary for growth. Emotions can run deep now, and kind, supportive words are needed.

Sunday 18th

How can you find a happy medium between duty and leisure time? Today feels like an 'all work and no play' day. How can you best serve your community and help others? Health can become a concern if you feel that you give more of yourself than you should.

Monday 19th

Jupiter is getting attention from both Venus and Mars today. Jupiter and Venus get along well and he helps her to develop anything that you value, such as money or belongings. Mars, on the other hand, is not happy with Jupiter, and is unable to move on with his exploration.

Tuesday 20th

Remember that Mercury is still retrograde. Today he is opposite Uranus, who will be occupying your career sector for some years to come. Be careful not to upset your boss. Vent with close friends if you need to complain about work.

Wednesday 21st

You may still be unstable in the workplace today, and there could be power struggles. However, with Venus in your area of love and money, you may be able to sweet-talk your boss into thinking you are due a rise.

Thursday 22nd

The Sun enters Scorpio today, which means you are likely to investigate intense emotions within your family of origin. Mother issues could surface now. Be careful of aggression and watch out for small accidents.

Friday 23rd

Wear your heart on your sleeve and spend time with a loved one today. The Moon and Venus are in a good connection to make the next couple of days sweet and romantic. If you are single, take some time to be nice to your shadow and treat yourself to something special.

Saturday 24th

You have a knack of getting what you want today, so ask for it. Spending time with someone special can be enjoyable. You will have a harmonious day ruled over by Venus, who is sweet-talking Saturn into relaxing the rules a little. Have fun.

Sunday 25th

Mercury is lost in the glare of the Sun, so you may find that you have nothing to say today and prefer to remain silent. The Moon moves into your sex, death and transformation sector, so sit back and watch the show.

Monday 26th

An easy flow of surreal energy is suddenly surrounding you, and it feels wonderful. You could be floating on cloud nine or away with the fairies. Getting high on life is prescribed for you, so make the most of this dreamy day.

Tuesday 27th

You continue to have that feel-good factor around you and it is quite intoxicating. You and your significant other are addicted to each other today too. Enjoy the ride and make sure you come back down to earth gently.

Wednesday 28th

Mercury is reversing into your communication sector. Although he likes being there, the reason for his visit is to ask you how you make yourself heard in friendship circles. Are you pushy or placid? At the same time, Venus also enters this area and will address the fairness of these friendships.

Thursday 29th

Today you will feel very passionate about a new project you have had in mind. You will want to get it off the ground but retrograde Mars is not in a position to add his energy to it. You will have to wait a while, so put it on the back burner.

Friday 30th

Here comes another day where your career is taking up more space in your head than anything else. There is nothing wrong with this. You might be putting your heart and soul into a work project, and want to be recognised for it. Quite rightly so.

Saturday 31st

A Blue Moon, the second Full Moon in a calendar month, occurs in your career sector today. This might reveal some startling facts about the workplace. Keep your eyes and ears open, and you may well learn something to your advantage.

NOVEMBER

....

Sunday 1st

The Moon in your career sector gets a helping hand from Jupiter in your daily routine sector. Work stress could get bigger, but in a way that will ultimately benefit you. There may be some disturbances at work or some exciting new developments. Keep yourself informed.

Monday 2nd

Even though it is just the start of the week, you feel the need to be out and about with friends. Social networking or post-work drinks could be just the things to ease you in gently. Saturn in your daily routine sector gives you the go-ahead.

Tuesday 3rd

The Moon acts as an anchor and holds Mars and Venus together, so it is a good time for dealing with the opposite sex and settling arguments. Travel and communication are highlighted for you today. Do you have a long-distance love interest? Could this be a possibility now?

Wednesday 4th

Mercury goes direct in your short journeys and
communications sector. It is time to apologise for things
that may have caused hurt. You can also now think about
travel without any disruptions or cancellations. You feel
a sense of moving towards your future and where you
are meant to be.

Thursday 5th

It is a dreamy kind of day, where you make plans in your
head and build castles in the sky. Feeling adrift from
everyone else, you want to stay in your comfort zone
physically but retreat into the fantasy world in your mind.

Friday 6th

You are still feeling the need to be wrapped in cotton
wool, but you have a sense of guilt about doing so. Your
rational mind kicks in and tries to pull you out if it. Stay
there a little longer if you can, and you will be ready for
action when you reappear.

Saturday 7th

The Moon moves into your sign today. How will you use
this energy? You are feeling needy, and may be stroppy
or throw tantrums if those needs are not met. You
can't always get what you want, so focus on what you
need instead.

Sunday 8th

Static energy will leave you pacing up and down your room wanting to roar but unable to. You feel frustrated. This will soon pass, so try to focus on one thing and see it through to the end. A sense of accomplishment is what you need now.

Monday 9th

This could be another testing day. Venus and Mars are in direct opposition and there will be a clash between the sexes or around issues regarding travel. This will be irritating and may see you spending too much money on pretty things. Put the wallet away.

Tuesday 10th

There is an intense urge for balance right now. A 'now or never' feel hangs over the day. You want to get something out of your mouth before the right moment passes. This could involve you taking a short trip to do so, rather than by emailing or texting.

Wednesday 11th

Being thorough is what is needed today. Pay attention to what money is coming in and what is going out. You will be thinking about how much you spend on yourself, as well as how much time and money goes out to others.

Thursday 12th

As the Moon moves into your short journeys and communications sector, she bumps into Venus and they talk about love, beauty and harmony. At the same time, Jupiter and Pluto are sitting together wondering what they can change in your work and service sector. They want to make something bigger and better.

Friday 13th

A mystery-solving Moon moves into your family sector and makes a connection to the Jupiter and Pluto tactic talks. You may find that this is about how you devote yourself to others, especially family. How might you transform existing duties and make them more worthwhile?

Saturday 14th

You will feel the sense of pressure lift as Mars goes direct in your travel sector. He wants to move forwards, but this has been a frustrating time in this area for you both. Things will pick up again and you will realise that you were stuck for a very good reason.

Sunday 15th

A New Moon in your family sector gives you the
opportunity to start afresh with issues pertaining to
mother, ancestry and family. As this all takes place in
Scorpio, the new starts could be something that go
deep and far back. You could find some gold in your
family history.

Monday 16th

Power and control issues are likely today, as Venus is
confronted by Pluto, who craves control. Venus will
probably win, and for you that means that these issues
could be about sibling rivalry. Keep your roar to yourself.

Tuesday 17th

Mercury has been diving deep into your family sector
but today he is opposite Uranus, so prepare for a
shocking revelation. Your mood will turn to the past and
thoughts of where you have been to get where you are
now will surface.

Wednesday 18th

Feeling stuck in a rut? Your need for action, adventure and
exploration is being hampered by a pull from the Moon
in your duties sector. What is holding you back from the
pioneering lifestyle that is attracting you now? This mood
will pass quickly, so just stay with your thoughts.

Thursday 19th

Emotionally, you may feel pulled in different directions today. This is a good opportunity to check in with your health and look at where your energy is going. There is a lesson to be learnt about who and what drains you to the point of exhaustion.

Friday 20th

Relationships, especially with significant others, are highlighted today. It is not an easy energy as the Moon is making uncomfortable aspects to Uranus and Mercury. Both of these planets can be unpredictable, and you or someone close could say or do something regrettable. Best to lie low and take it easy.

Saturday 21st

The Sun moves into your creative sector so it is time to play. You will feel more enthusiastic about getting out, making, playing, laughing and putting yourself on show. This is a favourable month for Fire signs like you. Venus brings harmony to your family sector too.

Sunday 22nd

You require depth in conversations today. Triviality just will not do. Partnerships can be explored and enriched with discussions about secrets and anything taboo. Sex, death and rebirth fascinate you, and you are eager to learn more about what makes another person tick. Have fun with it.

Monday 23rd

You may still be exploring mystical subjects today and, as the Moon joins Neptune, may be tempted to disappear off into an imaginary land. Choose a fantasy film or novel to get lost in, and write down any inspiring ideas you may find there.

Tuesday 24th

You now want to get out and conquer new lands. Other cultures will appeal, as will other religions. You have many plans in your head and feel upbeat and positive. Making a vision board or ticking off countries on a map could be a nice activity if you can't get away for real.

Wednesday 25th

Mercury is in your family sector, and is talking to Neptune in your sex, death and rebirth sector. Together, they are gathering information on family backgrounds. Secrets and lies can surface now. Intrigue is possible, but as it is in the past it is best left there. No finger pointing required.

Thursday 26th

Your get up and go has got up and gone today. Your emotional energy does not match your physical energy. You have needs to fill but you are held back by your daily routine and possibly health worries. You need an energy boost in a gentle way. Try a good belly laugh.

Friday 27th

Today we have Venus opposite Uranus, which is basically a fight between harmony and disruption. This occurs in your family and career sectors. These sectors can also be about the legacy you will leave, as well as the one you have inherited. Watch out for a financial matter that's about to erupt too.

Saturday 28th

Things can seem a bit surreal for you now. There may be some aftershocks that knock you off balance. Try to get grounded by eating, taking a walk or chatting to a trusted friend. Doing physical exercise will help too. Just remember to breathe.

Sunday 29th

You will want to get out and be sociable now. You need friends around at this time, if just to maintain some sense of normality. Being the centre of attention is not what you need, so try letting someone else have a turn.

Monday 30th

A Full Moon and partial eclipse in your social sector may make things a little unpredictable. This is actually a good thing, so go along with it and see where it leads. You may find something new and exciting is staring you in the face just waiting for you to say yes.

DECEMBER

· · · · · · · · · · · · · · · · ·

Tuesday 1st
You will begin December by listening to your heart
and its yearnings. Feeling creative and playful comes
naturally to you, but there is an added sense of
adventure too. You will wonder about the big, wide
world and what exactly is out there for you to discover.

Wednesday 2nd
You will have another one of those days where you
just want to be left alone and wallow in your dreams.
Switching off and taking a break will be good for you.
Shut your door, pull up the duvet and read a good book
or watch a film.

Thursday 3rd
Why is it that you will not allow yourself some free time?
Yes yours is a fire sign, but even a fire knows how to
burn quietly. Action is not favoured today as your heart
is not in it, but you have a habit of making yourself feel
guilty for standing still.

Friday 4th

The Moon moves into your sign today, helping you get your fire back. Mercury is in your creative sector and is whispering in your ear about projects he would like to see you do. He will start shouting loudly if you do not pay attention.

Saturday 5th

The Moon and Mars, both in Fire signs, give you the motivation you need to get on with things today. The only thing to watch out for is the Moon's uneasy connection to Uranus in your career sector. Be wary of possible unrest at work.

Sunday 6th

A positive flow of energy between Venus and Neptune brings harmony to your sex, death and rebirth sector. Shared finances also feature today and, as Venus loves money, this can only be a good thing. Just be careful that this is not one of Neptune's illusions.

Monday 7th

Money is on your mind again today, as the Moon moves into this sector. Some nice surprises may come your way in the form of gifts or innovative ideas. Work with this energy and allow yourself to feel pleased about whatever this brings. You deserve it.

Tuesday 8th

Everything is ticking along nicely now. Time management comes easily and you can fit in work, play and helping others. Being good to yourself by scheduling in a gym session or relaxing massage will really benefit your health.

Wednesday 9th

Catching up with friends and family via text message, social media or email will be the theme for today. You can bring harmony and balance within relationships, if you so choose. You have an easy-going manner and people will be drawn to your magnetic charm.

Thursday 10th

Venus helps you to relax some control issues that may have been going on in your family sector. This is likely to be where family members have been demanding your time and presence. Try not to hold on to anything that is a myth or an illusion.

Friday 11th

Emotional shocks are likely now in your family sector. Uncomfortable issues from the past come back to be healed. This is not your job, but if you use compassion you can be a great leader in this. If you are not directly involved, show integrity by keeping out of it.

Saturday 12th

The two female energies of the Moon and Venus sit closely together in your family sector. Listen to female voices. Mothers, grandmothers, aunts and sisters will have the knowledge and wisdom that you need to hear. Organise a pow-wow and listen up.

Sunday 13th

The Moon enters your creative sector and self-expression comes easily now. You can be centre stage, but do so with the leadership qualities that you possess. Being narcissistic and demanding is not going to get you anywhere. Laugh, sing and play. Shine in your glory.

Monday 14th

A New Moon in your creative sector can see you beginning an art project or endeavour that you put your heart and soul into. Venus and Jupiter are in a good connection, and will help this new project to be beautiful and grow in the way you wish.

Tuesday 15th

Venus steps into your creative sector so anything that you begin now has her blessing. This could be love, money or beautifying your home. The energy and motivation you need will be provided by Mars, while the ideas will come courtesy of Mercury.

Wednesday 16th

You could be decluttering today and making space in your life for new things to come in. There is a chance to follow your dreams and manifest something you have been longing to do. Creating a vision board may help you to focus, and see what needs to be removed before starting a new quest.

Thursday 17th

The Moon is busy today with Jupiter and Saturn. Jupiter, on the last degree of your daily routine sector, is urging you to think big before moving onwards. Saturn is making sure you have done all the research before moving into your relationship sector. This is a big time for you.

Friday 18th

Mercury, who is in your creative sector, is dazzled by the Sun today. You may experience a little brain fog, so use this opportunity to think with your heart instead. Sometimes going with your instincts is the best way forward. On the other hand, you may be overloaded with bright ideas and will want to write them all down.

Saturday 19th

Your inner world and outer appearance are in sync today, and you are able to express what is in your heart. Inner peace wraps you comfortably, and there is a glow around you that attracts people. Work with this. Meditation or yoga can help.

Sunday 20th

This is a big day in the heavens. Jupiter and Saturn are on the same degree in your love and relationship sector. This may be experienced as a 'push and pull' type of energy. Listen carefully and you might hear the lessons that they are trying to teach you.

Monday 21st

Today, the Sun and Mercury move into your daily duties sector. The next few weeks will be a chance to take a good look at your routine and give your health an overhaul. The winter solstice occurs in this sector too, so enjoy the darkness of the longest night.

Tuesday 22nd

You may be feeling on edge. You have a restless heart, coupled with an urge to get out and about. You need new initiatives to explore or fresh projects to start. Sit tight. The restlessness will pass and then you can move forwards.

Wednesday 23rd

You may feel some anger rising and will want to throw
things out the window, including any recent ideas
you may have had. This is due to uneasy connections
between the Moon (emotions), Mars (motion) and Pluto
(control). Manage the small things today and leave the
bigger ones for tomorrow.

Thursday 24th

You are eager to start building something. Could this be
your empire? You've had many new ideas seeding this
year and now feel they can be planted. Your career
needs to be reviewed or last-minute jobs completed
before the holidays. Take this opportunity to embrace
the forward momentum.

Friday 25th

Merry Christmas! Despite the holiday today, you feel
restless and would rather just get on with your new
plans. There is a lot of chatter going on about work and
the mundane jobs you do, sometimes for others. Leave
the angst and enjoy your family's company. Fathers and
sons feature greatly.

Saturday 26th

You can resume dreaming up your big vision. You have this under control, and know exactly what you want and how you are going to get it. This is something you are not going to let anyone else take over. Dream big, you deserve it.

Sunday 27th

Today, you can spend time with friends and tell them your new plans. You will be seen as innovative and unusual, and friends will want to join your happiness party. Be aware that you, and you alone, need to steer this ship, but that there is nothing wrong with gathering allies and sound advice.

Monday 28th

You will have a series of 'light-bulb moments' today. Ideas are coming thick and fast, and you can see the road ahead far into the future. This may only be in your dreams, but stick with it. Your determination is the factor that will propel you forwards.

Tuesday 29th

A Full Moon in your dreaming sector asks you to look back at the last six months. What have you managed to manifest without realising it? This may also be to do with family and especially mothers. A reward may be offered today or you could give yourself a well-deserved pat on the back.

Wednesday 30th

You may want to keep your thoughts to yourself today. Take some 'me time' and lie low. Venus in your creative sector is not very happy with Neptune in your sex, death and rebirth sector. She is seeing money spent on trivial items and does not approve.

Thursday 31st

Congratulations for getting through 2020. Planetary alignments were tough this year, but you did well. Any celebrating you do tonight can have a Scorpian theme to it. Secrets and lies may surface, which could be erotic and sexy. Have a good evening, but stay safe.

Leo

....

PEOPLE WHO
SHARE YOUR SIGN

PEOPLE WHO SHARE YOUR SIGN

Leonians have studded the stage, ruled the roost and brought laughter and fun into people's lives for decades. Whether they choose to be actors or are born/marry into royalty (or, in the case of Meghan Markle, both), Leonians shine in the spotlight. Discover the courageous and sparkling stars who share your exact birthday, and see if you can spot the similarities.

July 23rd

Daniel Radcliffe (1989), Paul Wesley (1982), Kathryn Hahn (1973), Monica Lewinsky (1973), Marlon Wayans (1972), Philip Seymour Hoffman (1967), Slash (1965), Woody Harrelson (1961), Jo Brand (1957)

July 24th

Turia Pitt (1987), Mara Wilson (1987), Elisabeth Moss (1982), Anna Paquin (1982), Rose Byrne (1979), Danny Dyer (1977), Jennifer Lopez (1969), Kristin Chenoweth (1968), Amelia Earhart (1897), Alexandre Dumas (1802)

July 25th

Paulinho (1988), James Lafferty (1985), Shantel VanSanten (1985), D.B. Woodside (1969), Matt LeBlanc (1967), Iman (1955), Estelle Getty (1923), Rosalind Franklin (1920)

July 26th

Stormzy (1993), Taylor Momsen (1993), Kate Beckinsale (1973), Jason Statham (1967), Sandra Bullock (1964), Kevin Spacey (1959), Helen Mirren (1945), Mick Jagger (1943), Stanley Kubrick (1928), Aldous Huxley (1894), Carl Jung (1875), George Bernard Shaw (1856)

July 27th

Winnie Harlow (1994), Taylor Schilling (1984), Jonathan Rhys Meyers (1977), Tom Kerridge (1973), Maya Rudolph (1972), Nikolaj Coster-Waldau (1970), Triple H (1969), Julian McMahon (1968)

July 28th

Harry Kane (1993), Cher Lloyd (1993), Soulja Boy (1990), John David Washington (1984), Alexis Tsipras, Prime Minister of Greece (1974), Lori Loughlin (1964), Hugo Chávez, Former President of Venezuela (1954), Jacqueline Kennedy Onassis (1929)

July 29th

Joey Essex (1990), Allison Mack (1982), Fernando Alonso (1981), Josh Radnor (1974), Wil Wheaton (1972), Sanjay Dutt (1959), Tim Gunn (1953), Geddy Lee (1953)

July 30th

Joey King (1999), Yvonne Strahovski (1982), Jaime Pressly (1977), Hilary Swank (1974), Christine Taylor (1971), Christopher Nolan (1970), Simon Baker (1969), Terry Crews (1968), Lisa Kudrow (1963), Laurence Fishburne (1961), Arnold Schwarzenegger (1947), Henry Ford (1863)

July 31st
VanossGaming (1992), Victoria Azarenka (1989),
B. J. Novak (1979), Emilia Fox (1974), Antonio Conte
(1969), J. K. Rowling (1965), Wesley Snipes (1962), Louis
de Funès (1914)

August 1st
Jack O'Connell (1990), Bastian Schweinsteiger (1984),
Jason Momoa (1979), Ryoko Yonekura (1975), Coolio
(1963), Yves Saint Laurent (1936), Abdullah of Saudi
Arabia, former King of Saudi Arabia (1924), Herman
Melville (1819)

August 2nd
Charli XCX (1992), Edward Furlong (1977), Sam
Worthington (1976), Kevin Smith (1970), Mary-Louise
Parker (1964), Wes Craven (1939), Peter O'Toole (1932),
James Baldwin (1924)

August 3rd
Karlie Kloss (1992), Charlotte Casiraghi (1986),
Evangeline Lilly (1979), Tom Brady (1977), James Hetfield
(1963), Martha Stewart (1941), Martin Sheen (1940), Terry
Wogan (1938), Tony Bennett (1926)

August 4th

Cole and Dylan Sprouse (1992), Crystal Bowersox (1985), Meghan, Duchess of Sussex (1981), Anna Sui (1964), U.S President Barack Obama (1961), Billy Bob Thornton (1955), Louis Armstrong (1901), Queen Elizabeth the Queen Mother, (1900)

August 5th

Olivia Holt (1997), Jesse Williams (1981), James Gunn (1966), Mark Strong (1963), Pete Burns (1959), Maureen McCormick (1956), Neil Armstrong (1930), Joseph Merrick (1862)

August 6th

Charlotte McKinney (1993), Ferne McCann (1990), Robin van Persie (1983), Vera Farmiga (1973), Geri Halliwell (1972), Michelle Yeoh (1962), Barbara Windsor (1937), Andy Warhol (1928), Lucille Ball (1911), Alexander Fleming (1881)

August 7th
Helen Flanagan (1990), Rick Genest (1985), Abbie
Cornish (1982), Charlize Theron (1975), Michael
Shannon (1974), David Duchovny (1960), Bruce
Dickinson (1958), Wayne Knight (1955)

August 8th
Shawn Mendes (1998), Princess Beatrice of York (1988),
Roger Federer (1981), Meagan Good (1981), Chris
Eubank (1966), The Edge (1961), Dustin Hoffman (1937),
Emiliano Zapata (1879)

August 9th
Bill Skarsgård (1990), Anna Kendrick (1985), Audrey
Tautou (1976), Gillian Anderson (1968), Eric Bana (1968),
Whitney Houston (1963), Michael Kors (1959), Melanie
Griffith (1957), Jean Piaget (1896)

August 10th

Kylie Jenner (1997), Brenton Thwaites (1989), Devon Aoki (1982), JoAnna García (1979), Angie Harmon (1972), Justin Theroux (1971), Suzanne Collins (1962), Antonio Banderas (1960), Juan Manuel Santos, Former President of Colombia (1951), U.S President Herbert Hoover (1874)

August 11th

Alyson Stoner (1993), Jacqueline Fernandez (1985), Chris Hemsworth (1983), Anna Gunn (1968), Joe Rogan (1967), Viola Davis (1965), Hulk Hogan (1953), Steve Wozniak (1950)

August 12th

Cara Delevingne (1992), Mario Balotelli (1990), Tyson Fury (1988), François Hollande, Former President of France (1954), George Soros (1930), Cantinflas (1911), Erwin Schrödinger (1887)

August 13th
DeMarcus Cousins (1990), MØ (1988), Sebastian Stan (1982), Alan Shearer (1970), Debi Mazar (1964), John Slattery (1962), Fidel Castro, Former Prime Minister of Cuba (1926), Alfred Hitchcock (1899), Annie Oakley (1860)

August 14th
Brianna Hildebrand (1996), Nick Grimshaw (1984), Mila Kunis (1983), Paddy McGuinness (1973), Halle Berry (1966), Emmanuelle Béart (1963), Magic Johnson (1959), Steve Martin (1945), Doc Holliday (1851)

August 15th
Jennifer Lawrence (1990), Joe Jonas (1989), Ben Affleck (1972), Anthony Anderson (1970), Debra Messing (1968), Melinda Gates (1964), Alejandro González Iñárritu (1963), Anne, Princess Royal (1950)

August 16th

Evanna Lynch (1991), Cam Gigandet (1982), Frankie Boyle (1972), Steve Carell (1962), Madonna (1958), Angela Bassett (1958), James Cameron (1954), Charles Bukowski (1920)

August 17th

Taissa Farmiga (1994), Austin Butler (1991), Thierry Henry (1977), Donnie Wahlberg (1969), Helen McCrory (1968), Sean Penn (1960), Robert De Niro (1943), Mae West (1893)

August 18th

Maia Mitchell (1993), Frances Bean Cobain (1992), G-Dragon (1988), Andy Samberg (1978), Edward Norton (1969), Christian Slater (1969), Patrick Swayze (1952), Robert Redford (1936)

August 19th

Ethan Cutkosky (1999), Christina Perri (1986), Melissa Fumero (1982), Fat Joe (1970), Matthew Perry (1969), John Stamos (1963), Gerald McRaney (1947), U.S President Bill Clinton (1946), Gene Roddenberry (1921), Coco Chanel (1883)

August 20th
Demi Lovato (1992), Andrew Garfield (1983), Ben Barnes (1981), Amy Adams (1974), Misha Collins (1974), David Walliams (1971), Fred Durst (1970), David O. Russell (1958), Joan Allen (1956), Robert Plant (1948)

August 21st
Bo Burnham (1990), Hayden Panettiere (1989), Robert Lewandowski (1988), Usain Bolt (1986), Laura Haddock (1985), Carrie-Anne Moss (1967), Kim Cattrall (1956), Kenny Rogers (1938), Wilt Chamberlain (1936)

August 22nd
James Corden (1978), Rodrigo Santoro (1975), Kristen Wiig (1973), Richard Armitage (1971), Adewale Akinnuoye-Agbaje (1967), Ty Burrell (1967), Honor Blackman (1925), Ray Bradbury (1920)

August 23rd
Jeremy Lin (1988), Kobe Bryant (1978), Julian Casablancas (1978), Scott Caan (1976), Ray Park (1974), River Phoenix (1970), Rick Springfield (1949), Gene Kelly (1912)